# atlan

## BOB QUINN

QUARTET BOOKS

LONDON   NEW YORK

First published by Quartet Books Limited 1986
A member of the Namara Group
27/29 Goodge Street, London W1P 1FD

British Library Cataloguing in Publication Data

Quinn, Bob
Atlantean.
1. Atlantis 2. Ireland—Civilization
I. Title
398' 42 GN751

ISBN 0–7043–2524–1

Typeset by MC Typeset Limited, Chatham, Kent
Printed and bound in Great Britain
by Nene Litho and Woolnough Bookbinding
both of Wellingborough, Northants

*This book is dedicated to Robert, Hannah,
Toner, Bairbre – and Miriam*

# Acknowledgements

The reason for this book is the existence of singers and sailors in Conamara. I thank them for their constant stimulus. The first glint of a perspective on the subject came from Desmond Fennell whose constant encouragement over the years is much valued.

John de Courcy Ireland's vast knowledge of Irish maritime matters was an inspiration. Several scholars, including Heinrich Wagner, Heinz Kiewe, John Allegro, Leo Henry, Joseph Raftery, David James, Gearóid MacNiochaill and Hilary Richardson may blush at the mention of their personal efforts to keep me on the straight and narrow. They are not in the slightest responsible for the result. The late E.G. Bowen was kindness itself. Michael Ryan was a patient and incisive devil's advocate. Chris Lynn, James Mavor Jr, D. Roy Saer, H. Cabillic, Daithi O h-Ógáin, Tom Dietrich, Paul Edwards, Peter Woodman, all made their erudition available. I received valuable information from Jean Le Du, Leslie Shepard, John Goodwillie, Charles Acton, Mary Beith, Esther Galbraith, Sean Hutton, Fred Johnston, Pat Sheeran and George Broderick. Practical help came from Mohammed Hassini, Vivienne Dick, Anne Cassin, Anne Simpson, Miriam Allen, Rhiannon Thomas, Lucy Helmore-Ferry, George Babawi, Muiris de Cogan, Patricia Donelon, Helen Quinn, Jean O'Hanlon, Peadar Lamb, Joe Comerford, and Alf MacLochlainn. There was encouragement from Kevin O'Connor, Denys Tollemache, John R. Hayes, Bearnard O'Riain, Pádraig and Máire de Bhaldraithe, Roisín Ni Mheára-Vinard, Igor and Pilar le Floch, Dáibhí Doran, Martin Ahearne, Mary Byrne, Tony Moylan.

My visits to Egypt were facilitated by Dr Makhlouf of the Egyptian Embassy; to Morocco by Ahmed Rayane. In Cairo, Brian O Ceallaigh was the most erudite and hospitable diplomat I have ever met. Micheāl O Cinnēide helped no less. The staffs of the National Museum and Library in Dublin, of the Chester Beatty Library, the British Museum, the Welsh National Museum, University College Galway were most courteous to me. As research for this book coincided with the making of the Atlantean films, I must thank RTE, S4C, RTM, ETV and Bord Scannán na h-Ēireann for their generous patronage.

# chapter one

The Chief Engineer of Ireland was not just angry when he saw what the upstart vicar had written: a lifetime's work was dismissed as 'the ravings of a bedlamite'. He, who had spent years studying the customs and antiquities of Ireland, who had mastered the obscure language of the people, who had even founded the periodical in which the criticism appeared, was accused of producing a 'fairy labyrinth of absurdity'.

The Chief Engineer was an Englishman. Like many others of his race he had developed such an affection for this small island and its people that it had inspired him to construct proof of their antiquity: not only was their language inherited from a mighty Eastern civilization but the people themselves were almost full-blooded Phoenicians. He had demonstrated beyond doubt that their famous Round Towers were the ruins of ceremonial monuments built by Eastern fire-worshippers. Who better than an engineer to analyse such structures? But this presumptuous vicar was dismissing all of that: 'such a tissue of Hiberno-Oriental adventures as never before appeared on paper'. The man even had the temerity to propose some ridiculous system of his own: the Round Towers had been built by Scandinavians; some of the megalithic tombs had been constructed by Danes; it was from these wild Northmen that the Irish were descended. Without the slightest command of Gaelic, the vicar presumed to ridicule the Chief Engineer's linguistic discoveries: the latter could not prevent the traditional Irish fables from 'sinking under their own imbecility'. It was completely preposterous!

The bitter argument between Charles Vallancey the engineer and Edward Ledwich the vicar was ironic for a few reasons. The former, an Englishman, was proposing a noble pedigree for the Irish; the latter, an Irishman – albeit with English antecedents – was declaring them barbarians. Each seemed to invoke the discipline of his opponent. Vallancey, whose discipline was practical, had used imagination to construct a religion-centred past for the Irish. Ledwich purported to be a man of God, yet used the rationalist tools of the Enlightenment to demolish it and erect a Pagan Norse context in its stead.

If Vallancey was right, the Irish were civilized before the English took over; if Ledwich was correct, and the Norse had colonized the island, then it proved that the Irish were doubly barbarian because everybody knew the Norse were uncivilized.

The dispute between Vallancey and Ledwich was, at the end of the eighteenth century, one of the topics of the day. Another theory – that Ireland's origins lay to the west – was put forward by the Frenchman De Latocayne who thought Ireland was the remaining fragment of a land mass submerged by the Atlantic in pre-historic times. In the late nineteenth century, this theory re-emerged in Ignatius Donnelly's *Atlantis, the Antediluvian Civilisation.* However, these theories that the Irish came from the north, south or east were never as widely accepted as the theory that they came overland from the east, that they were Celts.

It is widely held that the Celts migrated eastwards across Europe in the seventh and sixth centuries BC, though their origin is still a subject of debate. By the mid fifth century BC, the Celts had begun to colonize Britain and Ireland. The archaeological evidence does not indicate the extent of Celtic colonization in Ireland, the extent to which they replaced or mixed with the indigenous population. At the end of the nineteenth century the 'Gaelic Revival' supplied Ireland's need for an identity other than that offered by the increasingly unpopular English. The foundation of such groups as the Gaelic Athletic Association, the Society for the Preservation of the Irish Language, the National Literary Society and the Gaelic League helped establish firmly the theory that the Irish were Celts and helped focus the national feeling that led to the establishment of the Republic. The theories of Vallancey, Ledwich, De Latocnayne and others were dismissed as quaint: an orthodoxy was established which greatly impoverished Irish culture.

The sixteenth-century poet Edmund Spenser thought that 'it is certain that Ireland had the use of letters very anciently and long before England', but he was impatient with claims that the Irish were related to the Spanish: 'Of all the nations under Heaven the Spaniard is the most mingled and most uncertain; whereof most foolishly do the Irish think to ennoble themselves by wresting their ancestry from the Spaniards.'

If Spenser had read that marvellous libel, *The History and Topography of Ireland* by a Welshman named Giraldus Cambrensis, he might have torn his beard out. For here, using Irish literary sources, no less than five invaders are credited with an input to the race. They are, variously, a granddaughter of Noah called Cesara; a grandson of same called Partholon; a Scythian named Nemedus who held the country for 216 years 'and for 200 years afterwards the land was empty'; somebody named Dela who came from Greece and, finally, two brothers named Hibernus and Hermanus who came from Spain. To this list from other sources may be added tribes called the De Danann and the Fir Bolg.

Giraldus purveyed his account of the Irish in the twelfth century and seemed to have access to many sources for his research. But even if he had quoted accurately from these he would still have been in trouble. As Eoin MacNeill pointed out:

> The 10th and 11th centuries produced a school of Irish historians whose chief work was to reduce the old miscellaneous matter of tradition to unity and sequence. In dealing with the pre-Christian period they tampered with tradition in two ways; when they found definite elements of 'heathenism' they either cut these out or furbished them in a guise which they considered consonant with Christian belief. This can be shown to have been done consciously and deliberately.

Obviously revisionism is not simply a modern phenomenon.

Neither did scholarly habits seem to improve in later centuries. According to Seamus Delargy, a leading folklorist of his day, the scholars and literary men of Ireland whether they were Irish or Anglo-Irish wrote exclusively in English and were, in the main, 'completely ignorant of Irish and contemptuous of the language and the people who spoke it'.

Oddly enough, Vallancey, the most ridiculed of these scholars, seems to have been one of the rare exceptions. At least he went to the trouble of learning Gaelic. Seamus Delargy continues on a mournful note: 'The loss of the language over most of Ireland brought about the destruction of the oral literature enshrined in it, leaving a gap in our knowledge of Irish folk-lore which can never be filled.' This was a pity because, as scholars sometimes admit, the oral traditions of a people can valuably complement physical evidence.

Twentieth-century scholarship has lost the exuberance of the Vallancey–Ledwich controversy and seems to be governed by an orthodoxy imposed by 'the die-hard attitude of Dublin traditionalists', as John Philip Cohane put it: interlopers are discouraged from offering opinions in specialized fields. When a young American, Martin Brennan, dared to explain the famous Boyne Valley passage graves in terms of astronomy – ie they were solar laboratories rather than primarily burial places – he suffered an unprecedented savaging. It was, therefore, with a certain amount of trepidation that I began to research the subject of Ireland's connections with, among other places, North Africa.

I sympathize with the prudence of scholars – which is based on bitter experience. Too often their findings, carefully shrouded in ifs and buts, have been plucked out of context and used for crude propaganda purposes. The pleadings by Herder in the eighteenth century for the dignity of the German language and people was a reaction to the arrogance of the Frankish courts; who could have seen there the seeds of an Aryan nightmare in the twentieth century? Still unnamed chauvinists in 1912 took advantage of tentative archaeological-dating techniques to prove that one of the earliest examples of Homo sapiens had lived in England. He became known as the Piltdown man and was not exposed to ridicule for forty years.

The history of such hoaxes and fakery is entertaining but it has its serious side. It is noteworthy how often intellectual conclusions can coincide with the prevailing political and national ethos. Such conclusions can percolate down to become the conventional wisdom of the average person. Thus, the British will say that the reason the Romans did not invade Ireland was because there was nothing there worth conquering. The Irish will retort that the Romans were nervous about taking on such a redoubtable foe. The British will say that they sent the first man over to Ireland in Palaeolithic times; the Irish will say it's just as likely he came from the Continent.

The British will claim the Book of Kells for the north of England; the Irish grow indignant at such a suggestion.

In the island of Ireland itself a similar friction can be found. Northern scholars have traditionally pointed to a greater incidence of mesolithic flints in their area as evidence of the earliest habitation of the country. Their Southern counterparts will reasonably point out that if as much attention had been paid by colonist antiquarians to the South, a similar density might be found. However, a Northern archaeologist, Peter Woodman, recently investigated the flints in the North and came to the conclusion that they were not necessarily made later than their equivalent in Scotland, from where it had been suggested the first settlers came. Subsequently Michael Ryan, a Southern archaeologist, found material in Lough Boora which showed that the first settlers could have arrived in Ireland at almost any point on the east coast. Dr Woodman is presently working in the south-west of the island and is confident that he can find similar flints there. He has already pushed back by 2000 years the estimate of the earliest date at which people arrived in the Dingle peninsula in Kerry.

In other words, the 'truth' in these matters is simply a working hypothesis to be confirmed or denied by whatever new evidence is found. However, the fact remains that a traditional opinion on the entry point of the earliest inhabitants was based on the finds of antiquarians who had a vested interest in showing the North of Ireland was more advanced than the South – even 9000 years ago!

In fairness, the people most conscious of these grey areas are the scholars themselves; hence their prudence, but also their wrath when mere laymen intrude. It is akin to the relationship between Theologians and the Faithful. Robert Graves has written trenchantly on this subject from the perspective of the poet. 'That so many scholars are barbarians does not much matter so long as a few of them are ready to help with their specialized knowledge the few independent thinkers, that is to say the poets, who try to keep civilization alive. The scholar is a quarryman, not a builder, and all that is required of him is that he should quarry cleanly. He is the poet's insurance against factual error . . . the poet's function is truth.'

In terms of 'fact' it would, nevertheless, be interesting to plot a graph showing the correlation between the scholarly consensus in a society and the dominant political ethos that prevails at any given time. On a large scale, the relationship between Europe and say, the Middle East is a case in point. It is clear that the colonial experience has complicated the history of ideas here and significantly coloured the accounts. How much does the West owe to the East? Did ideas and cultures, even civilizations, move from East to West or vice versa? At one stage Mesopotamia and Egypt are credited with the beginnings of everything. At another, Europe is proclaimed to have had a separate and quite autonomous development.

These matters were once the preserve of amateurs – gentlemen who had the money and leisure to excavate at will, collect archaeological artefacts and speculate freely. They had not the scientific equipment to date their finds precisely. Even the advent of serious professional archaeology had its limitations. It was not until such techniques as tree-ring dating and carbon-14 techniques were refined that there was any hope of precision. But even these brought a serious problem. In the constant pursuit of certainty the archaeologists found themselves having to consult botanists, chemists, geologists, linguists, anthropologists and a whole range of other specialists. There was the nightmare that the new techniques radically altered some agreed dates by up to a thousand years which then challenged the entire canon of archaeological and historical faith.

As one scholar, Colin Renfrew, frankly stated: 'Once it is accepted that no model of the past can claim to be uniquely correct – any man is free to claim his own – it follows that no theory relating to past events can ever be final.' The expression 'any man is free to claim his own' is enough to send a shiver up the back of any member of the learned classes. Look at Luther and the trouble he caused. Look at Galileo!

But the reality of the matter is such that 'any man' is likely to be so intimidated by the complexity of matters that he will rarely try to construct his own model of the past. The honest seeker of the truth will find himself drowned in a sea of statistics, scientific jargon and opinions so qualified as to be useless. Even the solid common sense of the archaeologist in the field tends to be overwhelmed by the flood of information. There is a temptation to long for the ill-equipped antiquarians with their romantic and sweeping generalizations. As F.R. Scott once put it, 'the rain of facts that deepen the drought of the will', seems to have taken over.

Scholarship is constantly invoked to support cultural attitudes. Historians must sometimes despair at the use to which their findings are put. In the North of Ireland Protestants can point to the historical fact that the Catholic Irishmen in the

British forces put down the nationalist rising of 1798 in the North, where the rebels were actually Protestant; Catholics, for their part, can quote the Protestant leaders of the United Irishmen to support their nationalism. And everybody knows that the Protestant William of Orange had the backing of a Catholic Pope when he defeated the Catholic James at the Battle of the Boyne.

The Bible itself is one of the most abused products of scholarship. In the Middle East, Israel uses the entire Good Book to justify its existence in Palestine. The Palestinians hesitate to rely on the same source; all they have as evidence is half-a-million refugees. The Bible was used in the seventeenth century by an Archbishop Ussher of Dublin to prove that the world was created in exactly 4004 BC. Even today there are thousands of sincere evangelists relying on the book's authority to go to the opposite extreme and prove 'the end of the world is nigh'. No wonder the Catholic Church has traditionally discouraged the faithful from reading the Bible for themselves. In the secular field, the Irish, Norwegians and Spanish have scholar-backed claims that, respectively, St Brendan, Leif Ericsson and Christopher Columbus first discovered America. As usual, the claims of the 'indians' who were there before them all, are ignored.

No wonder scholars are so careful, so inclined to cloak their words in impenetrable jargon that few can misquote them, never mind understand them. This seems to be the effect of specialization which, in the sciences and the humanities, is approaching a point of absurdity. As the geographer and historian Estyn Evans pointed out: the most significant discoveries in future are likely to be found in the gaps between disciplines. An Irish archaeologist specializing in megaliths will refuse to give an opinion on North African tumuli. In the blinkered world of the specialist – however brilliant the individual – the human genius for making imaginative leaps is in danger of atrophying. As Robert Graves said: 'To know only one thing too well is to have a barbaric mind: civilization implies the graceful relation of all varieties of experience to a central humane system of thought.'

For fifteen years this writer has lived among and observed a living community in a 'remote' spot on the edge of Europe: Conamara in the West of Ireland. From this perspective, Europe looks different. So, for that matter, does the island called Ireland. Instead of being a distant and unimportant planet on the edge of a galaxy whose axis runs East/West, Ireland can be seen as the centre of a cultural area that is oriented North and South, is based on the Atlantic seaways and stretches from Scandinavia to North Africa. From such a perspective Vallancey and Ledwich may eventually be reconciled.

# chapter two

Midway up the west coast of Ireland there lies a region called Conamara. It occupies the area to the west of Galway city and forms the northern shore of Galway Bay. It is a much-visited part of this small island on the edge of Europe which protects England and Wales from the full force of the Atlantic while at the same time deflecting the warm waters of the Gulf Stream northwards to Scotland. Being on the western side, Conamara takes the brunt of the attack from the Atlantic. To this unpromising region I migrated many years ago.

When visitors to Conamara rave about the desolate beauty of mountain and bog, of lonely lake and moorland, it is clear to me that they have not experienced the place at all. They have been shepherded by some tourist brochure northward through a countryside that looks well from a bus – particularly because there are no people to clutter the view. They have been consciously steered away from the coastal region, South Conamara, the most densely populated region in rural Ireland. The northern section is beautiful, all right – but relatively unpopulated; the southern part is crowded and relatively untidy. In addition, the inhabitants speak a different language – Gaelic, show a disconcerting indifference to modern tourism and sing songs that fall uneasily on Western ears.

Conamara is about as far west as you can go in Europe. The people here are more familiar with Boston than Dublin. In the 1840s, a local man is reputed to have packed his entire family into a small boat and, with plentiful supply of salted pork, sailed away from the Great Famine to America – 3000 miles away. The incident serves to introduce the most significant and most overlooked aspect of Conamara and its people: their obsession with boats and the seas. They seem to be the only large and identifiable community in Ireland which realizes it inhabits an island. For certain reasons, rooted in the colonial experience, the Irish of recent generations have all but ignored the sea. Consequently, reporters on Conamara tend to overlook its predominant characteristic. In contrast to the rest of Ireland where boating is essentially a suburban hobby, a rich man's sport or part of the neglected fishing industry, the average Conamara person has a feel for the sea which is striking. On almost every Sunday in summer crowds gather in the various bays and harbours to celebrate the survival of their own traditional craft: the hucaer, gleoiteog, pucān and currach.

On festive occasions in Conamara the sense of history is sublimated to present enjoyment. The main attraction, apart from hotly contested rowing races, is the sailing competition. The most spectacular features the hucaer or 'bād mōr', literally 'big boat'. It has a massive oak construction, a dramatic tumblehome or belly, heavy sails of canvas and can be up to forty-five feet in length. The sight of seven or eight of these boats scudding along in a brisk wind generates great excitement on shore. On the boats themselves the atmosphere is tense. Some of the skippers may have had their ships in dry dock for a few days in order to grease the hulls – I have seen one skipper laboriously applying margarine – for minimum water resistance. The races were actually suspended for some years because of the depth of rivalry involved and the doubtful techniques occasionally used to win. One outlawed tactic was to send a sharp piece of flint whizzing across to rip into a rival's taut sail and thus deflate it. This was considered fair when a rival had cut inside and 'stolen your wind'.

In these races the satisfaction lay not simply in taking part. Winning was all and it was based on a sound economic tradition. These big boats were used for carrying turf from bog-rich Conamara to places that had none, the limestone islands of Aran as well as East Galway and Clare. Whichever boat reached the small harbours first made sure of the inside berth beside the quay wall. This made the unloading easier, saved hours of waiting and ensured the best price for the turf.

The tradition of this trade is annually commemorated on the first weekend in August when a fleet of the turf-boats, with large brown, black and red sails, sets sail from a pier in Carraroe and races across Galway Bay to Kinvara. However, this impressive sight is at variance with what one might call the prettiness and understatement of Conamara itself. It is hard to reconcile the massive beams and generous scale of the hucaeri with the intimate life-style and organic architecture that, up to recent years, the people themselves cultivated. It is as if all sense of grandeur was siphoned off from domestic life and channelled exclusively into these boats. Perhaps this was how the people showed their pride in themselves when in all other areas they were modest, even reticent. The small thatched cottages and tiny plots of land were undemonstrative. The fact that this life-style has been largely replaced with modern bungalows and cars, while dependence on the sea has diminished, indicates that the two aspects were interrelated.

Nevertheless, the presence and impact of the sea is still in the consciousness of the people. This expresses itself first in the physical environment: a series of islands and peninsulae hewn out by the Atlantic, the top soil stripped off by the gales which begin in September and sometimes do not let up till March. This indented coastline means that virtual neighbours, a half-mile apart, might have to travel twenty miles by road to visit each other. As against this, the presence of shops, post offices, pubs and travel agents on the remotest tips of these islands and peninsulae suggests that it was not always thus. The location of these services makes no economic sense until one stops looking through the windscreen of a car and realizes that the logical connection between these places is the boat.

Until quite recently, practically all commuting and transporting was seaborne. Water was not a barrier but a lifeline. Even social life – not to mention life itself – depended on the currach. On summer evenings young people would pile into these canvas boats, row to the next island or peninsula, dance all night and row home at dawn. There is sad evidence for this in the memory of occasional drownings. These were more likely if the indigenous brew – 'poitín' – was indulged in. Even in the context of this illegal drink, and the efforts to suppress its manufacture, there is evidence of the native regard for boats. 'Poitín' is made on small islands and beside freshwater lakes. When the still is raided, the natural escape route is over water. The local forces of law and order constantly bewail the fact that the powers that be will not supply them with a fast boat to engage in hot pursuit. Officialdom has still not realized that we are all surrounded by water. As a result captures are rare. So the Conamara person's respect for boats has, even in this case, a practical rather than a romantic basis.

This insight was of the greatest importance when I began to wonder about the strange music of the area: sean-nós singing. It is a pity the term is so imprecise: sean-nós simply means 'old style'. A pity, that is, for the uninitiated. Practitioners of the art and their dedicated audience know, with ferocious precision, what is meant by the term: an ascetic, unaccompanied form of solo singing which at its best has not succumbed to the emotional sogginess of pop music. It may not be too much to claim that whoever can be moved by the writing of Sam Beckett has the capacity to enjoy sean-nōs singing. In it, passion is pared away to reveal the extraordinary courage at the heart of the human being. Describing the most heart-rending events in his song, an intelligent performer's face will betray not one wisp of emotion. This singing defies comparison with the drawing-room tradition and its sentimental offspring. There are no dramatic high notes, no hushed tones, no build up to a pyrotechnical climax. Instead the singer will concentrate on minuscule decoration. In this there is an interesting analogy to be made with the art of manuscript illumination. At their best, singers like Darach O Cathāin and Sean Jack Mac Donncha could produce the equivalent of a page from the Book of Kells. Under a microscope some of the lines on these pages are miraculously fine. The art in them seems to be to conceal art. The satisfaction seems to be in the achievement rather than the acclaim. Similarly with the good sean-nōs singer. In performance the singer seems to escape into total introspection, as if communing with himself rather than the audience. In this way he draws the audience in to his semi-trance. As if to make sure he does not forget their presence, and also to reassure him of their support, one of the audience will grasp his hand and move it rhythmically in a winding action.

Inevitably, this extraordinary art form is withering. It is like a plant whose soil is being eroded. Most of the songs relate to the sea, be they accounts of lovers lost or terrifying storms. Consequently, as the maritime dependence of the people has lessened, so the musical form degenerates. This seems a more fundamental cause than that customarily offered: the decline in the use of spoken Gaelic. However, the singing is still the most popular event at the annual gathering of Gaelic speakers, the Oireachtas.

I encountered this music on the radio as a child in Dublin. It was quite alien to my urban ears which were accustomed to Italian opera, the lighter classics and the pleasant treacle of Bing Crosby. Indeed, sean-nōs singing was an occasional object of ridicule on stage and radio, being used as a symbol for an allegedly backward rural tradition which sophisticated urbanites should deride. In our house, sean-nōs was switched off. Twenty years later in Conamara it was impossible to exclude as it was the most popular form of musical expression and, as I learned, the basis of all traditional Irish music.

It was still difficult to enjoy. It defied all of the conditions I had been led to believe were essential to enjoy music: it did not lend itself to harmony; it had none of the simple rhythms of European classical form, nor the simpler rhythms of folk music. Also, it seemed to go on and on, endlessly. No matter how musical a person was – and I prided myself on my musical ear – it was impossible quickly to pick up the style and perform remotely well. Although Conamara people stated that it could be learned, they added, paradoxically, that it could not be taught. In other words, one would have to apprentice oneself to a singer and simply listen for years before acquiring the words, melodies, or styles of ornamentation. Even then much would depend on the performer's inventiveness because no two singers embellish a song in the same way.

It became clear to me that this form of singing

was an artistic response by a highly integrated community to a particular life-style in a long-settled environment. But this description does not match the conventional explanation of the origins of the people of Conamara. They are usually thought to be recent arrivals, descendants of the victims of Cromwell and his famous dictum: 'to hell or to Connacht'. The explanation matches neither the Conamara sense of identity, the people's ancient singing style, nor their highly developed tradition of boat handling and design.

If these people are the relicts of a forced westward migration in the seventeenth century, one would expect a hankering after, or at least a nostalgic feeling for, the lush grasslands of the east of Ireland. The reverse is the case. There is an almost complete indifference towards the capital, Dublin, and all its works and pomps. This attitude, in fairness, may simply be a reaction to the centralized power's treatment of Conamara as a kind of Gaelic museum. Whatever the reason, the discrepancy between stereotype images of Conamara, and the place as I found it, set up a state of mind which a sociologist might describe as 'cognitive dissonance': the facts as experienced did not fit traditional descriptions.

When I read descriptions of the place as 'lonely', 'remote', 'out in the wilds', I looked out of my window and saw fifty houses across the lake. On Sundays I saw traffic jams outside the church. Social life was consistently more intense and gregarious than in the average city suburb. Whatever the depressing results of American sociologists' sallies into rural Ireland, their findings simply did not fit Conamara. Whoever wrote the travel brochures about the place could not have spent much time here.

The social structure was so intimate, the channels of communication so efficient, that it was unwise to criticize a person in his absence: you were bound to be talking to a cousin. The traditional naming system was biblical: surnames were shared by so many that it was wise to have the person's first name as well as those of his father and grandfather. This must have caused people in official agencies to tear their hair out; was a sure way of confusing the computer. I found myself living in what was like a slightly foreign country. Luckily, I had no private means and was forced to work with the people. This meant learning the language – it was quite different from what I had been taught in school – which helped when I got down to studying sean-nōs singing. This became a kind of obsession.

On examination the music does not appear to be simply a survivor of a long-forgotten European tradition. The late and highly respected composer, Sean O'Riada, once spoke at length on the subject. In the course of three radio lectures he contended that sean-nōs was not European, nor could it be understood in that context; it was much closer to oriental forms. Irish art had never adopted the forms 'spawned', as he put it, by the Graeco-Roman renaissance. The best way to understand the music, he said, was 'to listen to it with a child's fresh mind'. In other words, dismiss all preconceptions. Failing that, he added, one might try to hear it in terms of Indian music. Sure enough there happen to be faint resonances in sean-nōs that would remind one of Indian music. And, of course, this would fit with the conventional Indo-European explanations of the origins of the Irish. However, when pressed as to how such music could have arrived in Ireland, O'Riada suggested it might have come via North Africa and Spain.

O'Riada was a classically trained musician, had composed film scores, wrote some of the most important symphonic music in Ireland, formed a folk orchestra whose influence was seminal in the popularization of traditional Irish music: the famous Chieftains folk group owes its origin to his inspiration. Not only was O'Riada an admired jazz pianist, his sophisticated company was much sought after. His analysis of sean-nōs should not be dismissed and his tragic death at the age of forty halted a fascinating line of enquiry.

Generally speaking, when Irish people listen to the music of the Middle East and North Africa they have an odd, aural equivalent of the sense of 'déjà vu'. Charles Acton, the music critic of the *Irish Times*, once wrote an extensive article on the subject:

> If one has listened for hours in the desert of an evening to Bedouin Arabs singing narrative epics with as many stanzas as a long 'aisling' (vision poem, in Gaelic) and then returned to Ireland and heard a fine sean-nōs singer using the same melismata and rhythm, one finds the resemblance between the two almost uncanny. So too, if one listens to 'canto jondo' (of Spain).

Mr Acton went on to say that he put the idea to an ethno-musicologist of authority. Her crisp reply was: 'Of course!' He concluded: 'The connections between the Arab lands and southern Europe, Spain and Ireland are, apparently, commonplace to scholars of her eminence.'

The Spanish connection was all right; Catholic Spain was always looked to by Irishmen as a possible saviour. Salamanca had educated thousands of Irish priests. Spanish Arch in Galway commemorates the busy trade between the two countries. Even the typical Conamara dancing called 'the battering' is the nearest thing possible to Spanish flamenco. But contact with 'the Arab lands'? Such an outlandish suggestion had never been made in my presence. It was completely at variance with conventional history which took all of the divergent characteristics of the Irish, both negative and positive, and dumped them into a rag-bag called 'Celtic'. The suggestion that sean-nōs had a respectably authenticated connection with the Arabs was startling. Not world-shaking, of course, as the music has a relatively small, loyal audience of aficionados and these principally located within the Gaelic-speaking areas of Ireland.

It is worth mentioning that an acquaintance spent three years in University College Dublin acquiring a degree in music without once hearing sean-nōs singing. Little attention is paid by musicians of the classical school to this 'folk-idiom', despite the fact that it is more subtle than a Scarlatti sonatina. I am aware of only one other serious Irish composer who has considered the form with insight. This is Dr Seoirse Bodley who wrote:

> The real oral tradition of sean-nōs is often obscured for many listeners by several factors. There is often confusion in the public mind between: (a) the genuine sean-nōs or oral tradition and (b) songs which are sung in Irish but without the style and without the traditional ornaments or tone quality.
>
> This does not mean that one objects to the songs of the Irish Language Revival, but that a clear distinction must be made between them and sean-nōs proper.

In the tightly knitted garment of Irish 'Celtic' culture there now appeared to me to be loose threads. If sean-nōs was 1) not European, 2) to be distinguished from the mainstream of 'Celtic' culture and 3) was alien to the majority of Irish ears, then where on earth did it fit? I spent five years tugging at these loose threads, with the usual consequences: the garment when unravelled was less a seamless jersey of pure 'Celtic' weave than a more interesting coat of many colours.

The first question to be asked was: how could there be any contact between two such apparently remote places – between Ireland and the Middle East, between two such different peoples – the Irish and the Arabs? They inhabited different continents, had profoundly different religious beliefs, were even racially different. One lived in the sun, the other on a misty island a thousand miles away.

Yet, listening now with more attention to those obscure radio stations that sometimes trespass on our wavelengths with strange music from North Africa, the possibility grew. For instance, the folk orchestra which O'Riada developed so many years ago consisting of fiddles, flutes, tin whistles, melodeons and a quite primitive drum called the 'bowrawn', did not, in retrospect, seem quite so remote from the distant strains of North Africa. Indeed, when I visited Iran in 1968 I recall being struck by the similarity between their 'classical' music and the O'Riada invention. At the time I attached little significance to it.

However, the goatskin drum which O'Riada rescued from obscurity in Kerry to become the basic rhythm section of most traditional Irish music groups, has its exact counterpart in the bindir, the drum of Morocco. It was interesting that O'Riada had, in creating a 'classical' folk music, unconsciously followed the example of the Arabs. Like them, he had respect for indigenous modes and techniques evolved over the centuries and which only required the sophisticated humility of genius to recognize and adapt. Admittedly,

O'Riada introduced a baroque note by using the harpsichord but he excused this as the nearest sound he could find to the great Irish harp.

In examining these matters a musicologist would get down to a detailed examination of the modes employed, the different scales, the instruments, chronology of these disparate manifestations of the same phenomenon. He would certainly soon realize – if he did not know it before – the debt European music owes to Arabic cultures: the violin's origin in the Middle East; the guitar's antecedent in the ud of North Africa; the influence of the Moors on the seminal Troubadour repertory of France; the excellent possibility that Europe may have got its first idea for a definite pitch notation from Arabic scholars. There have been vain efforts to keep sean-nōs in a respectable European context by comparison with Romanian and Hungarian musical idioms. Scholars who do this are invariably quite ignorant of the Islamic world and of the impact the Turkish Ottoman culture has had on those areas.

However, these details are overshadowed by the practical objection of the distance between Ireland and North Africa and the dangerous stretches of water between the two areas. Returning to Conamara, the objection does not seem insurmountable. Geographically, it is similar to the western seaboard of Europe: there is the same threatening Atlantic in common, the same cruelly indented coasts, the same peninsular layout. If the people of Conamara could develop such an unparalleled (in Ireland) tradition of seamanship to overcome the apparent social disadvantage of their physical environment, could the same principle not apply on the larger scale of the entire Atlantic coast of Europe? If Conamara regarded intervening stretches of water not as insurmountable barriers to social intercourse, but the very common means of achieving this intercourse, could not the same principle apply on a larger scale? Just as the Gaelic-speaking minorities in Ireland constitute a cultural archipelago in a sea of English speakers, could not the 'isolated' regions of Atlantic Europe constitute a similar archipelago, writ large? This would then include the Welsh, Bretons, Cornish, even the Galicians in a unity much more solid than that normally suggested for them. Morocco is also one such part of the Atlantic areas.

To most Europeans – but particularly to most Irish people – the idea of significant contact by sea is nowadays, in the presence of trains and cars and planes, a little quaint. This despite the incontrovertible fact that every single influence that reached Ireland in the past came by sea. The Irish mind is so paralysed in matters maritime that the boat between Rosslare and Fishguard or Pembroke, between Dun Laoire and Holyhead, between Larne and Stranraer – that is to say the shortest possible sea passages between Ireland and Britain – are about as far as the imagination can stretch.

Only in very recent years did the *nouveaux riches* of Ireland discover how relatively simple it was to sail their cruisers to the sunny climes of Marbella and the south of Spain. In fact, even the owner of a Conamara hucaer has recently taken to sailing his boat in summer to Santander. The latter is a highly appropriate event because, as sociologist Michael D. Higgins has pointed out: 'The migrant is the norm in coastal parishes. The deviant is the person who does not move.' This is borne out by recent finds on the remotest tip of the island of Leitir Mealláin in Conamara. Here Padraig Mulkerns, an amateur archaeologist, has found three groats from the reign of Henry VII (1490); coins identified as George II and George III; a Napoleon III piece; many Victorian pennies as well as a brass tap from a sixteenth-century wine butt.

Dr John de Courcy Ireland has almost single-handedly laboured for years to restore to the Irish mind a consciousness of its sea-girt position. In a lecture a few years ago he passionately declared:

> An tē mbīonn long aige, geibheann sē cōir uair ēigin. (He who has a boat invariably gets a breeeze.) A proverbial statement like that does not emanate from a people that is a landlubberly people. Long before the Irish language, or a Celtic language of any description came into this country of ours, we were a maritime people, and the blood that flows in every one of us here, every one of us in the country, is blood that came across the sea. I do not accept that because we have a reputation for holiness in this country, our ancestors were dropped from heaven. And you can go back to the very earliest moment in history and you find that the first people who came into our country came here by sea, and they laid the foundations of a maritime tradition that this country has, richer and older than almost any country in Europe.

At this point it would be helpful if, in the reader's mind, the image of Ireland as a remote and isolated place receded. Ideally, it might be replaced by the image of a traffic island, centre of a vast trade in boats up and down the Atlantic coasts from the Baltic Sea to the Straits of Gibraltar. As it happens, this is not just a figment of the imagination. Such, up to recent times, was the position of Ireland and there are many testimonies to this fact: instead of a nervous hedge-hopping to and fro between Britain and Ireland – spending the least possible time on the ocean waves – a picture emerges of the sea as, not a barrier, but an essential part of the multi-faceted culture of this island. It is appropriate that in Conamara, whence I derived this untypical perspective, there exists a more solid image of the idea.

The pucān – one of the four traditional craft of the area – has a quite unusual and distinctive sailing rig called the dipping lug, or lateen sail. This is the original sailing rig that revolutionized the art of sailing in the thirteenth century by making it possible to approach the wind from almost any direction. Hitherto the square sail had enforced long delays in port waiting for 'a fair wind', ie from astern. With the lateen a boat could be sailed almost directly into the wind and, by using the technique called tacking, could travel at the master's, rather than the wind's convenience.

Having sailed in a pucān right down the west coast of Ireland, I was familiar with this strange sail. But it came as a surprise to me to learn that the rig was an invention of the Arabs and that it was still in use in North Africa. From travelogues set in Egypt one can see the equivalent of the pucān in the dhows and feluccas of the Nile. Even in Tunisia, fishermen still use it. The pucān was, at one stage, the most popular fishing boat in Galway. Apart from the many in Conamara itself there was a considerable fleet working out from the Claddagh, in Galway city.

# chapter three

It is usual for a stranger to Ireland to be confused by the conflicting elements on this island. Dublin is a microcosm of this confusion. The city was founded by Vikings, overrun by Normans and developed by Anglo-Irish. Its first official language is Gaelic which is rarely heard in the city – few of the nation's leaders can muster more than one phrase in the language. The average Dubliner is more likely to get his or her opinions from the *News of the World* than from the *Irish Press*. The audience for American films was once, *pro rata*, the largest in Europe. Now British television dominates the citizens' tastes. The only regional accents dominant on the national broadcasting service come from the North of Ireland which is still part of the United Kingdom. Dublin, finally, contains a civil service more geared to running an empire than a small island.

Imagine being reared in this melting pot and being educated to believe you are something unique called a 'Celt'. This has been the experience of at least two generations of Dubliners. Still, generations of children in the Home Counties of England have been taught they are something called Britons; this, despite the fact that the only group vaguely entitled to that label are the Welsh. Similarly, to call the residents of Glasgow 'Scots' is really to say they are Irish. 'Scoti' was the original name for the Irish. It is all very confusing but it is, and has been, a functional confusion. The myth of 'Briton' built an empire; the myth of 'Celt' built a tourist industry – besides a good living for many scholars. Names are always arbitrary but over a long period they become reality; the word becomes flesh and people will eventually go to great lengths to prove they are, in reality, what they are called. Once the Irish adopted 'Celt' as a working title, they carried it to its logical conclusion. Not only did they base an insurrection on the idea, they founded an independent state as a result. To maintain consistency they were obliged to interpret the name racially and, as a result, any other strain that contributed to the personality of the island was regarded as alien, or at least a superficial intrusion.

A working identity is necessary for any people to throw off an intolerable colonial yoke. But, at a certain stage, the people must develop the confidence to dismantle the unitary myth that has served its honourable purpose and replace it with the diverse richness that lies beneath. Thus the suggestion that Ireland might have some connections with the exotic world of the Middle East was very attractive. Once the initial possibility emerged in the form of sean-nōs music, other clues followed. The early indications were superficial but exhilarating: even small things like the fact that the Arabic for Jesus is 'Issa', pronounced identically to the Gaelic 'Īosa'; in Egypt, a knife is 'sekina' which is like the Gaelic 'scian'; rosary beads, the badge of devout Irish Catholics, are a Middle Eastern invention still used by Muslims; and not only is the garment of the traditional nun Middle Eastern in origin – the word 'nun' itself is Egyptian.

When two strangers with a halting knowledge of each other's language meet, the first thing they do is compare vocabulary. A culturally egocentric European might be taken down a peg or two to realize the number of words he owes to Arabic: tartar, talc, almanac, alkali, borax, elixir. If he is interested in astronomy he will find many of the principal stars have Arabic names: Aldebaran,

Betelgeuse, Rigel, Vega, Altair. His mathematics would not proceed far without a smattering of Arabic: zero, sine, root, algebra. A chef is usually not aware that the Arabs brought him lemon, coffee, saffron, sesame, tarragon or that the French croissant comes from the Islamic symbol, the crescent. Many an uneasy crowned head of Europe was soothed by the Arab ud (lute) and where would Spanish music be without the Arab naq-quara (guitar)?

The European should remember that, without the Arabs, he or she might never have had a Renaissance, might never have learned about classical Greek thought. When Christianity in its enthusiasm eschewed the pagan Greek writers, the Arabs incorporated that learning into their own studies and preserved it until Europe was mature enough to appreciate it in the thirteenth century. The above points are readily accessible to the most casual enquirer and many educated Europeans are aware of them; culturally, Europe owed much to the Middle East, and Ireland – being loosely attached to Europe – must be similarly indebted. But was there anything unique in the case of Ireland? Whenever this question was raised, the image of Conamara and its people hove into my sight.

Some years ago a party of Irish musicians and dancers visited Libya. Among them was a Seosamh Mac Donncha who, after this experience, I should probably call Josie ibn Sean ibn Jack ibn Donncha. Josie is a sean-nōs singer from Carna, a village in Conamara famous for its singing style. He repeated to me his surprise at the pleasant reception his singing received in Libya. Without the faintest understanding of the words of the songs the Libyans gave him the attention he would normally only expect in Conamara. All became clear when Josie heard Libyan singing; to his surprise he found that if he closed his eyes he could easily imagine himself listening to a neighbour at home. It was hard to pin down the similarity, he said, but there were phrases here and there, perhaps a half-line now and again and an overall likeness in the style of ornamentation that made it all sound very familiar. His impression was confirmed by other members of his party.

When a Lebanese visitor to the Royal Irish Academy in the 1850s was asked to read from an ancient copy of the Qur'an which the academy possessed, he proceeded to chant it in the style of a muezzin. Coming up the stairs at the same time was Eugene O'Curry, a well-known antiquarian and native Gaelic speaker. As soon as the visitor stopped, O'Curry took up the refrain – but he continued in the strain of a Keener, or sean-nós singer of the West of Ireland. The people present said they could not distinguish between the two forms of chant or the words used. They came to the conclusion that the two forms were related.

Such speculation has a long pedigree and was quite prevalent in the nineteenth century. There were, even then, some aspects of the island's culture that did not fit into the classical European perspective, or lack of it. But others continually looked for more exotic explanations. What I found remarkable was the apparent haste with which this speculative line was dropped in the early years of this century. Its abandonment coincided with the adoption of 'Celtic' as a badge of identity.

Speculation such as this in the nineteenth century did not happen in a vacuum. Orientalism became a lasting obsession for educated Europeans of the time. In Dublin, second city of the British empire, it was an interesting distraction. The Grand Tour to the Middle East was highly desirable. One man-about-town, Buck Whaley, wagered that he could visit Jerusalem and be back in his club – à la Phineas Fogg – within a specific time. He succeeded and pocketed a clear £7000. Another gentleman was so impressed by his trip to Egypt that he built a miniature pyramid on his estate in Mayo; it is still there. Coincidentally, not far from this 'pyramid' were found the famous Turoe and Castlestrange stones. These are intricately carved in what is described as La Tene, ie 'Celtic' style, and are constantly invoked to demonstrate such a past for Ireland. I suggest that the designs might just as easily be described as 'arabesque'.

The old dispute between Vallancey and Ledwich was revived at an open-air lecture in Clondalkin, Co Dublin in 1866. Two valiant orientalists, Messrs Palmer and Darling, challenged the members of the Royal Irish Academy together with the 'antiquarians of Ireland generally' to come and hear their proofs that the Round Towers had an Eastern, Phoenician origin. They stated that: 'Traditions existing in this country derived from Eastern fable, manners and customs substantiate the analogous evidence between the habits and predelictions of the Irish and Eastern peoples. The Patterns and Pilgrimages, Particular Holy Wells and Fountains, the celebration of La Beal-tinne, the Irish Ullagone, the lighting of fires on St John's Eve, the Baalist names of bridges, towns, mountains, brooks, rivers & co.'

Still at the stage of finding the origin of sean-nōs singing, I wandered into the Chester Beatty Library in Dublin. This contains the greatest private collection of oriental manuscripts in the world. It was bequeathed to the Irish nation by the eponymous Canadian millionaire. The collection illustrates the history of civilization from about 2500 BC to the present time and therefore attracts as many foreign scholars as it does ordinary Irish citizens.

The curator, David James, was a fluent Arabist

and was intrigued by my interest in finding musical connections. Sadly, he could not help much in this area. However, if I was interested, he said, he had just published an article in which he compared Islamic art in the form of book illumination with the Irish equivalent. His article detailed surprising affinities between an illuminated Qur'an produced in Baghdad in the tenth century and those products of the golden age of Irish art: the Books of Kells and Durrow.

The Ibn Al-Bawwab is the only surviving manuscript in the hand of a famous Arab calligrapher. It is preserved only a short distance away from Trinity College, Dublin, where the Irish Book of Kells is kept.

Using this Qur'an and a facsimile of the Irish books, David James demonstrated the points of coincidence. The prominence of the design known as interlace was the most obvious; the central 'tree of life' symbol was also traceable in both books; the similar geometric composition of certain pages was striking. He emphasized that there were no exact likenesses but even he was intrigued that the two areas, Ireland and the Middle East – at opposite ends of Christian Europe – should have, as he put it: 'expressed spiritual and metaphysical ideas by means of an art which was either wholly non-representational, abstract, or in which the human element was subordinated to anti-naturalistic concepts'.

In other words, the Christians of Ireland and the Muslims of the Middle East were, at approximately the same period, expressing their opposing beliefs in similar ways.

I had, for a moment, the wild hope that the Arabs might have directly influenced the Irish in this art. But this was dispelled by the fact that the Books of Kells and Durrow were produced two centuries before this particular Qur'an. Still, there was the indisputable fact that both schools of illumination were clearly influenced by the visual repertoire of Egypt, Syria, Iran and Central Asia. This was predictable in the case of the Muslim book but I was pleasantly surprised to hear the same principle applied to the Irish books. Further, I decided that the emergence of a Christian art form – of which these Irish books were the most distinctive – and an Islamic form that resembled it, could not be a simple accident. There must be a connection. The only tentative suggestion that David James had for me was something called 'Coptic Egypt'.

This was the point at which my simplistic categories began, fortunately, to crumble. Were not all the people of North Africa and the Middle East called Arab? Yes, but only because they speak the Arabic language. There are Arabic-speaking Jews and Christians, too: the Copts in Egypt, for instance. They at one time spoke Egyptian – a distinct language – but since the ninth century they have adopted Arabic. All that remains of their original language is that used in their liturgy.

This was all very confusing. In the midst of investigating the origins of the Irish, a doubt emerged as to who and what the Arabs were. Ironically, about this time, a piece of physical evidence surfaced to illustrate the problem precisely. I learned about a strange brooch which had been found in a bog in Ballycotton, Co Cork, many years ago. Although it was made in the shape of the Christian symbol – the cross, the inscription on it was in Arabic: 'Bism'llah' (In the Name of God).

How did such a brooch get to Ireland? The British Museum, which now looks after it, gave the following explanation: 'The brooch dates from the reign of Charlemagne (768–814) and was manufactured somewhere in his Empire, but under the influence of Anglo-Saxon metalwork ornamentation. One can only guess how this piece came to Ireland, perhaps in the luggage of an Irish ecclesiastic visiting one of the great monasteries such as Corbie, which flourished under Charlemagne's patronage, or more prosaically, brought in by a Norse trader or raider.'

I had the temerity to pick a few holes in this explanation. First, was it likely that anywhere in the Christian Empire of Charlemagne – locked in bitter strife with the Muslims who controlled Spain – a craftsman would risk inscribing one of the commonest expressions of the 'infidel' on the holiest symbol in Christendom? Second, it overlooked the existence of the Christian Mozarabes of Spain who lived very comfortably with their Islamic masters; they even fought beside the Arabs when Charlemagne and the Franks entered Spain in the eighth century. These Christians might happily have tolerated the Christian symbol with the Islamic invocation. Further, there was always direct maritime contact between Spain and Ireland. As to how it got to Ireland: the prosaic afterthought, the Norse raiders, seemed to me the most appropriate for my thesis, so I opted for it.

In the period in question the Norse moved comfortably throughout the Atlantic reaches of Europe. They were familiar with the riches of the Islamic world. In 859, two Vikings called Hastings and Bjorn started a voyage from western France which took them down the coasts of Spain and Portugal, through the Straits of Gibraltar – where they must have encountered the Muslim navies intent on blocking the route. The raiders passed through to attack Italy, call on Egypt and return by the same route. They fought the Muslim navies again at Medina-Sidonia in Spain and reached home safely in 862. In the course of their adventure they attacked Asturias, Seville, Catalonia and the Balearic Islands – all Muslim strongholds except

Asturias. These daring marauders even wintered on the Camargue. With such activity going on down the Atlantic coasts of Europe and into the heart of Islamic civilization, it seemed feeble to credit Anglo-Saxon craftsmen with the design, or Irish ecclesiastics with the provenance of this Muslim artefact in Ireland.

Meanwhile, I began to discover more connections between North Africa and Ireland. An excavation took place in Eamhain Macha, or Navan Fort, which is a few miles from Armagh City. A friend of mine mentioned that a Barbary ape had been found on the site. But Barbary apes are associated with Gibraltar and have been there only a few centuries, their natural home being North Africa. The excavations put the remains of the Navan ape at around 500 BC. The date was indisputable because pieces of the animal's skeleton were found in different parts of the site and could not have been inserted under the oldest layers of stratified material. This was confirmed by Chris Lynn, the archaeologist whose job it was to collate the findings.

The ape, whose remains are in the British Museum, may have been somebody's pet. But how could it have travelled to Ireland from such a distant place? Had it come in the luggage of a Celt from central Europe, via Britain, of course? This was the route attributed to practically every unusual feature of Ireland. The Barbary ape was an awkward detail, another of those anomalies that do not fit the respectable version of Irish history.

The puzzle was compounded by a literary reference. This occurs in a play by William Butler Yeats called *Deirdre* which is a tragedy set in a mythological Ireland of 2000 years ago. The action takes place in the court of King Conchubhair which was located at Navan Fort where the Barbary ape was found. At the same time as the play was being performed in the Abbey Theatre, Dublin, modern archaeologists were operating in Navan Fort. In the play, to my amazement, I heard references to Libyan dragonskins – Libyan mercenaries. These dark-skinned fighters had apparently been hired by the frustrated old king to guard his interests. What on earth were Libyan mercenaries doing in the North of Ireland over 2000 years ago? Was it some hard-bitten soldier who, to remind him of his Mediterranean home, kept an ape as a pet? And how had he and his companions found out there was employment for their deadly profession on an island at the edge of the known world?

Yeats explained none of these puzzles; he had not, of course, invented the basic theme. The saga of Deirdre and the Sons of Uisneach are part of the Heroic literature of Ireland. The archaeological evidence shows that an impressive centre of activity existed at Eamhain Macha in the North of Ireland. As in all so-called 'myths' there was a central core of truth.

Some scholars have suggested that accounts of Heroic Ages contained in the oral tradition of a people are the result of invasions by people of a higher civilization. To accommodate the culture shock of an incursion on a large scale the victims weave stories in which eventually their own ancestors become the heroes. It is a kind of historical revenge. As a result, scholars can spend their lives trying to extricate the facts of invasions from the imaginative web in which they are embalmed. The historically documented invasions of Ireland are fairly straightforward: the Normans in the twelfth century, the Tudors in the sixteenth, the Vikings in the ninth and tenth. Beyond those dates – and possibly in the gaps between – there have been many permanent callers to the island. The furthest south to which anyone reliably attributes any kind of invasion is Spain. But there are historical incongruities, such as the Barbary ape, which suggest wider influences.

In the epic literature of Ireland there are many exotic references to places beyond Europe. For instance, in the *Táin Bó Cuailgne* (the *Cattle Raid of Cooley*), there is a reference to one of the heroes sporting a helmet 'do chumtach ingantach tiri Arabiae .i. crīchi na Sorcha' which means: 'of the wonderful workmanship of Arabia, ie the land of Syria'. The hero's charioteer is described as wearing a cloak which Simon Magus had made for Darius, King of the Romans, who had in turn given it to the King of Ulster et cetera. This king, Conchubhair, was the same king credited in the play *Deirdre* with hiring the Libyan mercenaries and whose court included a Barbary ape.

These exotic allusions are explained by scholars as much later interpolations in the text. That is to say that the original texts were written down in the seventh or eighth centuries but the scribes of the eleventh and twelfth centuries introduced new references learned, presumably, from crusading contacts with the Middle East. I was later to discover more on this subject. For the present it seemed one should attribute all connection with the Middle East to a series of literary and cultural accidents combined with a vivid imagination.

The unusual wealth of Irish epic tradition was simply a local re-working of universal myth; the Irish were great story-tellers, not averse to bending the truth a little; they had simply adapted travellers' tales to their own needs; the mound of dirt at Eamhain Macha they had turned into a palace; a hillock in Co Meath was 'Tara of the Kings'; these items were testimony to the marvellous Irish imagination but they were really based on Greek mythology and, where that did not fit, on a 'Celtic' source. In other words, even in their imaginative life, the Irish were locked into Europe – Barbary ape or no Barbary ape, Libyan mercenaries or not. Was there any escape from this academic strait-jacket, any way of showing that Ireland was open to and received formative influences from other than the Graeco-Roman world? The only escape route apparent to this particular 'scholar' was the sea.

# chapter four

Grāinne Mhaoil, or Grace O Malley, was a pirate queen of the sixteenth century. She controlled much of the west coast of Ireland from her castle fortress on Clare Island in Clew Bay, Co Mayo. The castle still stands and her coat of arms is still visible on the wall of the island abbey. When, in 1593, Grāinne decided to make her peace with England's Elizabeth I, she did it in style. Dismissing the idea of travelling overland to London, she sailed down and around the west and south coasts of Ireland, across the English Channel, through the Straits of Dover and up the Thames to Greenwich. It was probably her way of showing the Queen that she was no ordinary petitioner. It may also have been that the supposed perils of the deep – fogs, storms, other pirates – did not exist for her. At any rate, it shows that she was quite at home in the dangerous waters surrounding the British Isles. It was the sea that had enabled her to preserve freedom of movement for forty years.

It was only a few years later that the last of the Gaelic aristocracy in Ulster realized that they could no longer maintain their stand against the English. They decided on exile. But the O'Neills and the O'Donnells did not take the short route to Scotland; they piled their families and goods into ships in Lough Swilly and sailed the long way round to the continent. Similarly, the Wild Geese – the remnants of the broken Irish armies in the late seventeenth century – sailed out from Limerick to places as far away as Cadiz.

When the merchants of Galway were amassing their considerable fortunes to turn that port into the second largest on the island, they did not rely on trade with Dublin or London. They sent their wool and hides to Spain and received wines and silks in return. So strong and long established were their commercial links with the far south that the burghers even had a system of mutual foster-age with their counterparts in Spain. The crime for which the infamous Judge Lynch hung his own son was the unforgivable one of murdering a Spanish youth who was in the judge's own care.

The defeat and wreck of the Spanish Armada in 1588 does not appear to have interfered too much with this trade. Four years later, the Lord Deputy was still naming Spain as the chief cause of disorder in Ireland. He attributed this to the immense trade between the two countries. In 1625, Sir James Perrot, Governor of Galway, described the town as 'next to Spain and trading with it'. This odd perspective – the west coast of Ireland being nearer to Spain than to England – is confirmed by an Arab map. On it, Ireland is clearly shown as lying to the south of England. This is not simply bad cartography. It illustrates how Ireland was perceived by sailors and is in the clear tradition of 'portolons', the earlier written instruc-tions by which mariners had traditionally navi-gated. For most of its history, Galway looked to the sea and to Spain. In 1834, a traveller named H.D. Inglis wrote the following:

> Galway, the capital of the wild west, is a large and on many accounts an extremely interest-ing town. I had heard that I should find some traces of its Spanish origin; but I was not prepared to find so much to remind me of that land of romance. At every second step I saw something to recall Spain to my recollection. I found the wide entries and broad stairs of Cadiz and Malaga; the arched gateways with

the inner and outer railings and the court within – needing only the fountains and flower vases to emulate Seville. I found the sculptural gateways and grotesque architecture which carried the imagination to the Moorish cities of Granada and Valencia. I even found the sliding wicket, for observation, in one or two doors, reminding one of the secrecy, mystery and caution observed where gallantry and superstition divide life between them. Besides these Spanish resemblances, Galway has a more Popish aspect than any other Irish town!

However, to limit Irish maritime contacts to Spain alone would be a mistake. The seas around Ireland teemed with strangers. Pirates in the sixteenth and seventeenth centuries frequently assumed command of the waters between Ireland and England. In the south-west on 7 August 1626, a French merchantman was ignominiously chased into Berehaven by a 'Turkish' pirate. In 1627 a pirate named Campane is reported as taking shore leave in Killybegs, Donegal, where he was 'always drunk and with loose women'. In 1608, a Venetian had already visited the coast of Cork and reported it was one of the chief nests of 'pirates'.

The image of Ireland as a traffic island was never more apt than at this period. But the maritime orientation went back a long time. As James Kenney put it: 'From the years when the great forests succeeded the post-glacial steppes down to comparatively recent times, the easiest and most frequented way was the sea, or rather the sea coast, and Ireland's position is most favourable.'

As long ago as the second century AD, the geographer Ptolemy was able to name sixteen tribes in Ireland, all of them on the coast. Ptolemy was an Alexandrian. From whom did he get his information if not from Mediterranean sailors who had ventured into these cold northern waters and, on arrival in Alexandria, were obliged to lodge a copy of their portolons in the Great Library of Alexandria? This library, tragically destroyed by fire in 642, no doubt contained numerous accounts of voyages in and beyond the Mediterranean.

Another potential source of records for early contacts with these islands was also totally destroyed much earlier: Carthage. The Romans wiped out almost all trace of the Carthaginians' first recorded voyage to these northern islands. These North Africans had originated in the Lebanon and built up a trading network second to none in the Mediterranean. Their second home, Carthage, beside present-day Tunis, was founded in 813 BC as a colony of Tyre and Sidon. It outgrew its founding cities and became the third largest city in the ancient world. I also sauntered through these ruins, besieged by guides who wanted to sell me 'authentic' Phoenician coins and lamps. But there was plenty of evidence, beneath the subsequently built Roman villas, of the Phoenician custom of infant sacrifice. Hundreds of tiny coffins made of stone were stacked in the basements. It was as if the Romans has purposely left this evidence of an ugly custom so that future generations would think them right to have razed the city.

According to the historian, Pliny, and the poet Avienus, a man from Carthage voyaged through the Straits of Gibraltar and explored the Atlantic coasts to the north. The Carthaginians certainly had a base on the Atlantic coast of Spain called Tartessos and it must have seemed logical to them to see what lay further north. The man, Himalco, is credited with reaching Armorica – now Brittany – and describing the skin-covered currachs which are still in use in Wales and Ireland. A people named 'gens Hiernorum' (the Irish) and a place called 'insula Albionum' (England) are mentioned in references to his voyage which suggest that he reached these areas, too, and paved the way for the exploitation of Cornish tin.

At the same time as this man was sailing northwards, his fellow North African Hanno was sailing south, around the coast of Africa. He was hoping to emulate the feat of a Phoenician ancestor who in 600 BC had circumnavigated Africa on the commission of the Egyptian King Necho. This man appears to have succeeded, according to Herodotus, because he reported that, as they sailed westwards (round the Cape of Good Hope, presumably), the sun was on their right. This could not have happened in a northern hemisphere. Though Hanno only succeeded in getting as far as Sierra Leone, it still indicates that these North Africans, as early as 425 BC, were familiar with extensive stretches of the Atlantic coasts.

There is no doubt that to these men this ocean was a vast and unknown quantity. They had the idea that it was a kind of huge river flowing around the known world of the Mediterranean. If the world was flat, for instance, as many believed, there was to them a serious danger of being blown over the edge. Still, they considered the sea to be safer than land. This, despite the fact, as experienced sailors have told me, that the Mediterranean is prone to sudden and ferocious storms. These same sailors have emphasized that they would rather sail in the Atlantic than in the Mediterranean. It is more dangerous to hug the coastline than to venture on an ocean; apart from unexpected breakers there is less leeway should an onshore wind rise strongly.

Navigation was in its infancy. In unknown waters the sun and the stars were the only guide. If on emerging from the Straits of Gibraltar you head north towards Cape St Vincent you are, in effect, in the open Atlantic. The easiest star to locate in the sky is the North Star which is indicated by the pointers of the Great Bear, Ursa Major. From Cape St Vincent, if you follow that star, you will be led safely and directly to the south and west coasts of Ireland. It was the Phoenicians who taught the Greeks to find this North Star using even the guidance of Ursa Minor.

There was good reason why the Carthaginians would want to venture on the Atlantic seaways. They had indeed blocked the Straits of Gibraltar in 600 BC to protect their valuable silver deposits at Tartessos on the Atlantic coast as well as to monopolize whatever rich mineral resources lay further north. The Mediterranean was, for centuries, divided between the two peoples: the Greeks controlled the eastern and northern shores, while the western and southern shores were dominated by the Carthaginians. But the Greeks had founded and controlled Massalia – now Marseilles – thus giving them an overland route to the Loire and thence to the tin deposits of the British Isles. The Carthaginians were, therefore, forced to seek a different route to this raw material, necessary for mixing with copper to make bronze weapons and implements. The uncolonized waters of the Atlantic seaways were theirs for the taking or, at least, the traversing and they made sure the Greeks had no access to this route. It would be centuries before a Greek from Massalia named Pytheas dared to pass through the Straits, enter the Atlantic and explore the sea-route to the British Isles. This voyage is better recorded than that of the Carthaginian, Himalco, mainly because Pytheas had more prolific historians on his side, both Greek and Roman.

Ironically, although the Phoenicians/Carthaginians invented the alphabet, their exploits are the least recorded. This is partly because they were traders rather than conquerors, less interested in writing glorious histories than recording prosaic transactions; partly because their curving script, I am told, was harder to carve on stone than the straight lines of Roman numerals; mainly though, it was because their records must have perished when Carthage, their nerve-centre, was wiped out by Scipio Africanus in 146 BC.

Carthage perished, North Africa changed, Romans, Greeks and Vandals came and went, empires rose and fell in the following 1500 years. But, extraordinarily, this seagoing contact between North Africa and the British Isles persisted throughout all these centuries. The most dramatic evidence of this occurred one balmy summer's night in 1631 when the town of Baltimore, West Cork, was rudely awakened by pirates from Algiers.

All, all asleep within each roof along that rocky street,
And these must be the lovers with gently gliding feet.
A stifled gasp! A dreamy noise! The roof is in a flame.
From out their beds and through their doors rush maid and sire and dame,
And meet upon the threshold stone the gleaming sabre's fall
And o'er each black and bearded face the white or crimson shawl,
The yell of 'Allah!' breaks above the prayer and shriek and roar –
Oh, Blessed God, the Algerine is Lord of Baltimore.

The ballad *The Sack of Baltimore* was written 200 years later by Thomas Davis, an Irish Protestant Nationalist. The object was to show how heroically the Irish resisted these 'savages' from North Africa. He got most of the details wrong. The ballad can be taken as a metaphor of how history is written.

The term 'Algerine' – from Algiers – was interchangeable with 'Turk'. It was indiscriminately applied to the many privateers who dominated the Atlantic coasts from Iceland to the Mediterranean. The Spanish Main, the Barbary Coast are all terms that emanate from this period. Algiers was under Turkish rule at the time and along with Tunis, Tripoli, Salé and other ports of the North African coast was an organizing centre for what respectable people called piracy but which was simply the ordinary 'cut and thrust' of commercial maritime activity. The picture depicted by romantic histories, novels and Hollywood epics completely overlooks the highly structured nature of this trade. On 17 June 1631, two ships from Algiers landed during the night at Baltimore, a quiet seaside town. They ransacked Baltimore and took the entire population – 163 souls – back to North Africa.

> Oh, some must tug the galley's oar and some
>     must tend the steed,
> This boy will bear a Sheik's jibouk and that a
>     Bey's jereed.
> Oh some are for the arsenals by beauteous
>     Dardanelles,
> And some are for the caravans to Mecca's
>     sandy dells.

Although captives from raids like this sometimes ended up as slaves, they had other uses, too. Their captors placed them in four categories: as labourers (men); as companions or concubines (women); as a source of income, ie tradesmen for hire; and as a step towards Paradise according to

Muslim belief – small boys who could be 'converted' and thus add to the new master's store of grace. But all these were secondary to the prime aim which was ransom. This was the most lucrative aspect of the trade and is probably the main reason why captives were treated so well – despite contrary reports. As early as 1618 an Irish woman had a royal licence granted so that she could beg for funds to retrieve her husband from North Africa. These were the bread-and-butter captives, ordinary people. Occasionally, there was a bonus, as when Lord Inchiquin was captured off Portugal in 1659. It took six months of delicate negotiations for him to be released in exchange for the handsome sum of 7500 crowns.

It has been elsewhere remarked that a number of the inhabitants of North Africa have red hair and blue eyes. Nineteenth-century historians claimed they were the descendants of captives from Ireland. Whatever about that entertaining idea, Baltimore will not support it. With the possible exception of five people, all the hostages from this town were, in fact, English. This is because Baltimore was what is known as a 'planted' town, occupied by settlers; the Irish lived outside. Nevertheless, like many places on the south and west coasts of England and Ireland, Baltimore was regarded as a watering place for what were termed 'pirates'. It was certainly a centre of smuggling. This was a normal, respectable means of building a fortune in areas like this. It is illustrated by the fact that the family of Daniel O'Connell the Liberator achieved prosperity although locked away in the fastnesses of Kerry. They did it by 'importing' luxuries. Smuggling, in those days, had no stigma attached; it was a reasonable way of avoiding the oppressive tax laws of England.

One can assume there was a comfortable accommodation between the disenfranchised Irish and the pirates. As it happens, the man charged with piloting the pirate boats into Baltimore was named Hackett, a 'papist' from nearby Dungarvan, Co Waterford. Guilty or not, the man was hanged for the crime. It might not even be too much to speculate that Baltimore was considered a fair target because it was not inhabited by the native Irish. Then, few towns were. In this light, to a considerable proportion of the population – at least on the coasts – privateering must have been a quite justifiable activity. Only the minority who agreed with, and had a stake in, the European rulers' plans for distributing the wealth of the world could have frowned on this entrepreneurial spirit.

A European sense of righteousness towards these freebooters from North Africa must also be slightly blunted when it is realized that at the same time as the Barbary corsairs were plaguing Europe, English and French pirates were doing precisely the same in the Caribbean. It should be remembered that Francis Drake and Walter Raleigh, of whom British schoolboys are taught to be inordinately proud, were both experienced and successful 'pirates'.

It seems reasonable that, to North Africans, the rich vessels of European merchants should be treated as fair game. A fine service industry was built up on the Atlantic coasts to employ the many not yet absorbed in the tentacles of centralized power. There had to be what, in criminal parlance, is termed a 'fence' – a disposer of stolen goods and a market place for the captives. North Africa, being Muslim and therefore antipathetic to whatever rules of the sea that Christian Europe might proclaim, was the obvious centre. The ports of that part of the world became the regulators of a large and healthy commerce.

One of the ironies of this trade is that some of

the most successful captains of these North African-based pirate ships were themselves European in origin. In fact, the leader of the Baltimore expedition was a Dutchman. A fellow countryman of his, Jan Jensen from Haarlem, became such an outstanding success at the game that he achieved the title of 'Rais', equivalent of admiral.

Whatever one thinks of these privateers, they were magnificent seamen. Three Algerian ships could sail as far as Iceland in 1627, raid the capital and still have the energy and skill to navigate home with 300 captives. They must also have been masters of the art of naval warfare. Between the years 1613 and 1621 they took 447 Dutch, 193 French, 120 Spanish, 60 English and 56 German ships and brought them to Algiers as prizes.

There was a strict apportionment of the booty. In 1633 the rates were as follows: in Algiers, twelve per cent went to the Pasha – it being at least nominally controlled by Turkey – and one per cent went to maintain the mole or sea barrier that protected the city's harbour from surprise attack; one per cent went to the holy men attached to the city's mosques; forty-three per cent was divided between the ship's captain and its owners – who could be a group of citizens – and the remainder was allocated to the crew in order of rank.

John de Courcy Ireland has found many examples to show how this trade impinged on Ireland:

In February 1641 the Rev. Devereux Spratt of Tralee, Co. Kerry, was sailing for England from Youghal in the ship of one John Filmer of that town, but Algerian corsairs took their vessel while still in sight of land and carried them off to Algiers. Spratt expected a fate worse than death but was quite well treated, stayed to preach to the captives in Algiers (even) after his ransom came.

But Dr de Courcy Ireland adds that, in exactly the same year, the Viceroy Wentworth was being credited with wiping out piracy off the coast of Ireland. 'Evidently,' the researcher says, 'the Viceroy's intentions have been mistaken for facts.'

In reality, it took until 1843 for the combined British and American navies to put an end to this cultural exchange called piracy. They described their action as 'imposing European trading practice' which simply meant establishing their own monopoly. The involvement of America indicates how widespread was the influence of the corsairs. The Salley Rovers, from Sale in Morocco, were often active as far away as the banks of Newfoundland and the coast of Nova Scotia.

In Baltimore a couple of years ago a local resident invited me to see his newly acquired treasure. It was a large ivory tusk, found locally by a diver a few days beforehand. It was an appropriate trophy for a town that has a significant link with North Africa and this significance was realized by its possessor – a Breton. It shows what a reticent archivist the sea is, holding its peace for years and then releasing a tiny detail of evidence to jog our memories.

As a footnote to this episode it should be mentioned that the Irish were not simply passive in this impressive traffic. A scholar of the period has told me that among the 'Algerines' who operated off Howth in the Irish Sea, there was a pirate named O'Driscoll. He was certainly no Turk.

The maid that Bandon gallant sought is chosen for the Bey.
She's safe – he's dead – she stabbed him in midst of his Serail;
And when to die a death by fire that noble maid they bore,

> She only smiled – O'Driscoll's child – she
> thought of Baltimore!

The point of treating the North African corsairs in such detail is this: the regular traffic between 'isolated' coastal areas of these islands and North Africa has been practically ignored in the history books. The fact that freebooting ships could airily sail up and down the Atlantic reaches of Europe carrying goods and people – no matter how illegitimately – year after year, would have reflected badly on those charged with controlling such traffic as well as on the European powers who supposedly divided the world between them.

For at least 300 years – from the sixteenth to the nineteenth centuries – there was unofficial, possibly sporadic, but, from my point of view, significant contact between these islands and North Africa. Grace O Malley, as a pirate queen, clearly had more in common with the 'Algerines' than with the Queen's navy. Oddly, when she married her second husband, Richard Bourke, the contract stipulated that either party could, after one year, end it simply by saying 'I dismiss you'. This form of divorce had more in common with the Muslim faith than with the rigid tenets of Christianity. Naturally, evidence of contact in earlier times is more piecemeal. There is the belief that Columbus called in to Galway to collect stores and crew for his trip to America. The Portuguese certainly collected seamen from the western coastal towns of Britain and Ireland.

A more obscure legend is contained in the story of St John the Almsgiver, patriarch of Constantinople in the seventh century. In this there is a reference to a large Alexandrian grain ship voyaging to 'Britain' and exchanging wheat for gold and tin. A maritime legend that can be taken fairly seriously is that of St Brendan who is always referred to as the Navigator. He is claimed by the Irish as having been to America before Leif Ericsson. This is based on the mediaeval story called *Navigatio Sancti Brendani Abbatis* which existed in over 100 different versions. St Brendan is reputed to have lived at the end of the fifth century and the story appears to be a compendium of all the tales of wandering Irish missionaries of the following centuries. The earliest date to which the actual writing of the story is attributed is 800 AD.

The Vikings admitted that when they reached the Hebrides, the Faroes, even Iceland, they found the Irish had been there before them. These places are logical stepping stones on the route to North America as Tim Severin showed in 1976 in his re-enactment of the saint's voyage. Mr Severin is a specialist in testing the physical possibility of historically attested voyages. He showed, among other things, that references to strange natural phenomena in the *Navigatio* could have their equivalent in existing geographical features. He instances the Faroes as perhaps being the 'island of sheep' referred to in the text; the volcanoes of Iceland might be what were described as 'Fiery Mountains'; huge icebergs might be what were referred to poetically as 'Columns of Crystal'.

He also admitted that several places in the text were much too loosely defined to be capable of identification but that, as the *Navigatio* might include references to many voyages, in many directions, this was not unreasonable. For instance, there was some disagreement about the significance of the term 'Eastern Beach' which, in the context, means 'Eastwards' but which is a strange direction to follow if one is looking, as Brendan was, for the Promised Land in the West.

What principally interested me were the parallels between the adventures recorded in the *Navi-*

*Navigatio* and those of another sailor – Sindbad. The equally legendary voyages of this voyager constitute almost a separate block of stories in the *Tales of the Arabian Nights*. The first coincidence concerns Sindbad's crew landing on an island which turns out to be a sea monster. Exactly the same thing happens to Brendan's companions when they light a picnic fire on a small islet; it turns out to be the great whale, Jasconius. Another item is Sindbad's encounter with the great bird, the roc. In Brendan's account this becomes a flying gryphon. There is also the blinded giant who throws great boulders at Sindbad as he and his companions escape on a raft. This becomes, for Brendan, the natives of an island who throw fiery lumps of slag at them as they try to get away on their frail craft.

Both Sindbad and Brendan discover island paradises, see monstrous fish, find underground palaces and meet strange people. The similarity between the two voyages is particularly note-worthy because they are attributed to the same period (the ninth century) and happened to repre-sentatives of cultures apparently separated by geography and religion – Ireland and the Middle East. The relationship between the two works is as curious as that already noted between Irish and Islamic manuscripts. This coincidence tends to be underplayed by scholars of the classical school who attribute practically everything to Greeks and Romans first, and, when that does not fit, to the Indians and Persians. The Rev. Geo. Fyler Town-shend, MA, in a nineteenth-century edition of the Sindbad stories does not even give the Arabs credit as the originators of the tales. He attributes the credit to Plutarch, Aelian, Diodorus Siculus and Pliny – anybody but the Arabs. However, as A.A. Aleem – the Egyptian scholar and ocean-ographer – recently demonstrated, many of the wonders detailed in Sindbad could be related to existing biological phenomena in the Indian Ocean. These, when experienced by early Arab mariners, were interpreted in fantastic forms.

What is not easily explained away is how a writer in the ninth century – long before the Crusades – on an island in the North Atlantic could have had access to the literary wealth of the Middle East, be so familiar with it as to plagiarize it and issue a similar story in a Christian and Irish disguise. Surely everything could not be explained away by reference to twelfth-century copyists with a penchant for Middle Eastern embellishment? Certain light might be thrown on this matter by considering the Islamic domination of Spain which began in 711 AD and continued for 800 years – longer than England controlled Ireland and, coincidentally, about the same length of time as the Carthaginians were there, a thousand years before. That fascinating aspect I would investigate later. Meantime I was, in a manner of speaking, still at sea.

If there was any substantial influence from North Africa and the Middle East on these North Atlantic areas it had to come a long way by sea. If one could establish a continuity of voyaging between the two areas, from pre-historic times to the present, one could then reasonably attribute otherwise inexplicable features of Ireland to a more exotic origin than, say, Britain or continental Europe. I was fairly confident that this maritime possibility had been consistently ignored by armchair historians. North African pirates came here. Before them, the Carthaginians. The Vikings, having braved the northern seas to set up colonies in Ireland and greatly influence the island, were certainly not intimidated by the milder southern waters; they sailed to Egypt and back. There was even a suggestion by R.D. Barnet, a reputable maritime historian, that a Phoenician design used by the Egyptians was the basis of a Viking galley with its high prow and stern. There is a carving of such a boat, found during excavations in Dublin, which is certainly reminiscent of Egyptian carvings. Some scholars have even noted rock carvings at Newgrange in Ireland which echo these designs 2500 years ago!

The Irish monks were well-known seafarers, albeit not quite so organized as the Vikings. They tended to let the wind blow them where it would, rather like religious pollen, hoping to blossom on whatever bleak coast they landed. That, at least, is the impression they gave King Alfred when three of them landed in Cornwall. They declared that they merely 'wished to go into exile for the love of God; they cared not whither'. A scholar named P.W. Joyce posits three other monks in Carthage in the seventh century who were Irish. Two of them were called Baetan and Mainchine, respectively, and they wrote 'in elegant Latin, wonderful things of the Sacred Scriptures'.

These details tend to be regarded as exceptions: historians tend to ignore events that do not fit their theory. The Vikings are a classic example of contrasting versions of history. Traditionally, they were considered to be only a temporary, if painful, intrusion on the quiet land of Erin. In Irish history lessons these intrepid adventurers were described only through the eyes of their victims, the monks. Naturally only their depredations were mentioned: they were fierce pagans who arrived in their longboats, descended on the monasteries, pillaged the sacred vessels and books and disappeared back to Norway. The wealth of the monasteries made them an obvious target for marauders and warring Irish kings plundered monasteries before the Vikings. The Ulster Cycle records Irish attacks on monasteries in 757, 789 and

793 before the first Viking attack in 795. By 823, the Vikings had circumnavigated Ireland, attacking points all round the coast; they built shelters at Annagassan, Louth and Dublin, thereafter establishing settlements. The Ulster Cycle mentions the loss of thirty boats on Lough Ree in 756 and other incidents showing that the Irish had substantial fleets. At first the Irish were unable to retaliate against the marauding Vikings but later defeated them at sea in 856 and 926 and mounted raids on Viking settlements in England and the Orkneys in 913 and 941, respectively.

The 'settlements' of the Vikings became the first cities of Ireland. Dublin was the centre of the earliest Viking state recorded in the history of Western Europe. The Vikings named Wicklow, Wexford, Waterford, Arklow, Dalkey, Lambay, Howth, Leixlip, Skerries and many other places. They gave Ireland its first minted coin. They influenced its famous metalwork. They gave the north and the east a clinker tradition of boat-building (the men of the west use a carvel structure in their seagoing vessels).

It was taught, traditionally, that when Brian Boru defeated the 'Vikings' in 1002, they all piled into their boats and fled back to Scandinavia. Some of their warlords may have done so; but these people had been in and out of Ireland for two centuries. Many had become Christian, raised families in Ireland, fought beside, as much as against, the various factions in the country. On their own terms, as well as the terms of the period, they were as integrated into the population of the island as any 'native'. It is only through the quite recent and artificial construct of a homogenous people or nation that the Vikings of Ireland could be viewed as alien. The 'Celts', by the same logic, must at one stage have been alien. So, also, must even Christianity have been at one stage a novelty.

It is always the political urge to force a unified national image that causes certain categories of people to be excluded arbitrarily from credit for forming a people's culture. The settlers called Vikings contributed much to the multi-faceted personality of an island located in the centre of a busy north/south sea route.

# chapter five

There is a mountain in Wales, much frequented by hill-walkers and pony-trekkers, which boasts the strange name: Cadair Idris. The word cadair, like the Gaelic 'cathaoir', simply means 'chair'. The word Idris is a fairly common personal name in Wales. For centuries, kings and saints of the Muslim world of North Africa also have been called Idris. I visited the shrine of one such saint in Morocco. It was in a town called Moulay Idris perched on a hill within sight of the old Roman town of Volubilis. The shrine itself was considered so sacred that Christians were not allowed to enter, so, when I say visited, I really mean I stood outside and wondered. The Idris in question had founded a dynasty in Morocco in the seventh century – about the same time as Idris the Giant, a magician and astrologer, was reputed to have lived in Wales. Unfortunately, topographical names – those attached to rivers, mountains and features of the physical environment – tend to be much older than recorded history. If there was any connection between Cadair Idris and Moulay Idris it must have been long before Idris the Giant or the Muslim saint.

Generations of Irish people have passed through Wales without giving it much thought. They have been emigrants from Ireland bound for London. As the *Shamrock Express* usually passes through Holyhead and Bangor in the dead of night, they do not see much of this delightful country. A cup of British Rail tea on a windy platform at midnight is no introduction to the Welsh. As that had been my only experience of the country I decided to visit it formally this time, going by the southern route from Rosslare to Fishguard. This was the same route by which the Anglo-Normans came to 'civilize' the Irish in the twelfth century.

The topography of the country was quite familiar. It was battered here by the same Atlantic that shaped Conamara. Further north was less dramatic on the coast but the Welsh mountains made up for it. I met the late E.G. Bowen of Aberystwyth University who had noted the same North African connections as myself and had applied them to Wales. He had also been studying and writing about the Atlantic seaways for years. Not only did he not dismiss my speculations as ridiculous; he supplied me with ammunition. He brought scholarship to support the historical incongruity that I, in my ignorance, had intuited: that traditional history was based almost exclusively on literary evidence from classical writers who were not concerned with what they deemed 'peripheral regions'; the Roman Empire was built on a network of roads; it was inevitable that ancient and more recent authors should have concentrated on the land and rarely described the movements of coastal peoples.

What had happened to change the idea that 'the sea divided and the land united'? Archaeology was the key. E.G. Bowen was primarily a geographer but he thought as a historian. This, to me, seemed paradoxical until I realized that the physical context of an event is almost as important as the event itself. Man does not do his deeds in an ecological vacuum, does not build his shelter or manufacture his tools without direct reference to his environment. The movements of peoples should be capable of being traced by the artefacts they leave behind. If they leave a trail of broken pottery as they migrate, this is much more reliable evidence of the migration than that contained in written accounts based on tales handed down, although the latter must not be dismissed completely.

Similarly, if artefacts are found in very different places, but are clearly of identical manufacture, some kind of cultural contact can be assumed between these places, no matter how remote from each other. If a chart is plotted showing the relationship between these various finds you can make a good guess at the extent of a culture's influence, the routes it travelled and how it travelled. As always, such a plotting of finds is tentative and entirely subject to whatever evidence might emerge in the future. What was of interest to me was that E.G. Bowen, as well as Cyril Fox, Gordon Childe, O.G.S. Crawford and other eminent archaeologists, had applied this cartographical principle to the Atlantic seaways. They had come to the conclusion that, in distant times, the seas around Ireland were 'as bright with neolithic argonauts as the Western Pacific is today'.

I had a number of enthusiastic sessions with Professor Bowen – a short, lively old man. He warned me that his ideas, for instance, about the progress of early 'Celtic' Christianity were unpopular in Dublin. His approach was defiantly sea-based. He had little time for the classical perspective of ideas moving slowly and ponderously overland to reach the peripheral areas of Europe and the British Isles. His vision included a host of seafaring monks moving from peninsula to peninsula by sea, then carrying their light boats over the established paths to the next stretch of water. The jewel in his argument was the Cathedral of Dewi Sant, or St David, patron saint of Wales. This massive building is located at the tip of the Dyfed peninsula, rising impressively and surprisingly from a marshy valley, the Vallis

Rosina. It is the last thing one expects to find in such a 'remote' spot.

Such a foundation had to be located, even 1400 years ago, in what was considered to be the centre of the area served by it. If this were so, then half of Dewi Sant's parish consisted of sea. Most of the parish calls must have been conducted by boat. It was similar to what I had noticed about Conamara – the peninsular setting of shops and post offices. The position of this, the premier shrine of Wales, on such a peninsula implied that the original founders were seafarers. How they arrived at this place in Wales was debatable and whence they came even more so. It seemed ludicrous to suggest that they had got their inspiration from London and travelled through the dangerous land of southern England. They must have come by sea. From where?

A photo I acquired from the cathedral gave a clue. This shows a gathering of bearded dignitaries surrounded by their acolytes taken in the grounds of the cathedral in 1920. It was the occasion of celebrations to mark the disestablishment of the Church in Wales. They came from the East, from Nubia in Egypt, from Alexandria, too, from Jerusalem, and the Russian and the Byzantine churches were also represented. It stated clearly that the Welsh saw their traditional religious ideas extending further than the bounds of Western Christianity. It suggested that the Welsh were more aware of, and more willing than the Irish, to acknowledge their connection with, and debt to, the East. Was it their way of saying that the first carriers of this religion to Wales had also bypassed Europe initially?

In the church of St Mary's in Haverfordwest I was directed to a sculpture which represented a pilgrim. This female figure was lying down and by her side was a scallop shell, indicating that she had completed the journey to Santiago de Campostella, then the second shrine of Christendom. It was quite normal for the devout people of the British Isles to travel by sea from places like Plymouth directly down the Atlantic coasts to visit this shrine in Galicia, Spain: another example of the normality of long sea voyages undertaken by thousands of people over the centuries.

The love spoons found in Wales are fine specimens of folk art. Little attention has been paid to their origins, though it has been suggested that the custom of offering a carved spoon as a proposal comes from Scandinavia or Germany. However, in a town called Azrou in central Morocco, where exquisite wood carving is a feature, I came across a man carving love spoons. He used the same clever motif of chain-links fashioned from a single piece of wood. In Cairo, I was shown wooden spoons and forks carved with at least as much care as the Welsh versions. I wondered why the love-spoon custom should be automatically attributed to northern Europe. The frequency of rope and cable and anchor designs on them indicate that sailors passed the tedium of long voyages by carving these spoons. I could suggest that Welsh sailors had picked up this custom from their long voyages to the warm south but, as one expert has said: 'Since in its simplest form there occurs a basic similarity among most expressions of peasant art, these influences may be more imaginary than real.' However, the collection of love spoons in St Fagan's folk museum at Cardiff show that this activity achieved a standard far beyond the definition 'simple peasant'.

In the folk museum in Cardiff there was also an account of a traditional game called bando. It was played with a stick and a ball and featured two teams with an indeterminate number of players on each. It was clearly related to hurling before the latter became the national game of Ireland. Bando died out in Wales in the nineteenth century. There was a game called takourt played in Morocco at that period which was similar. It was outlawed by the French authorities on the grounds that it was 'très brutal'. The Irish game similarly affects the squeamish. Fortunately, it has survived its critics to become one of the fastest and most graceful games in the world.

In the National Museum in Cardiff there was a strange little model boat with what looked like eyes painted on the prow. It was called the Caergwyrle Bowl and somebody said it had Phoenician connotations. It was attributed to the Bronze Age and was more evidence of a maritime concern in those distant days.

In Anglesey, North Wales – the scene of the native people's last stand against Caesar's forces – there was plenty of archaeological evidence for contrast with Ireland. One site – Barclodiad Y Gowres – had designs which were described by archaeologists Powell and Daniel as 'mostly the disintegrated remains of a human figure, derived from those in Iberia'.

Other parallels, they said, were to be found in Morocco and on the Niger, while the resemblance between the multiple arcs on stones from Pola de Allande, Asturias, and menhirs at Tondidaro on the Niger was also to be found on Iberian bone idols. Such an openness to possible African connections was very refreshing to me, particularly as these designs were acknowledged to be related to their equivalent in Ireland. There must have been much to-ing and fro-ing on the Irish Sea up to a thousand years ago. Up to then, it is maintained, Welsh and Gaelic were mutually intelligible languages. South of Anglesey is the Lleyn peninsula, which has the same name as Leinster, across the Irish Sea. There has always been friction between scholars as to who is indebted to whom as far as names and language is concerned. Did the Irish colonize Wales or vice versa? Is Gaelic a late derivation of Welsh?

Some place names in Wales are distinctly Irish. Cilgerran on the River Cardigan is such a name. It commemorates the Irish Saint Ciarān. The village retains the use of what an archaeologist confusingly calls a 'palaeotechnic artefact'. This is simply a canvas-covered coracle, a diminutive boat in which big men still hunt the salmon on the River Cardigan. These are descendants of the boats that Himalco the Carthaginian described so many centuries ago. The fisherman kneels in front of the boat, facing forward and, with one small oar, literally drags himself through the water. Just across the Irish Sea from here, on the Boyne near Drogheda, exactly similar boats were used by the mussel fishermen. On the coast of Conamara a longer version, the currach, is used; this has a sharply upturned prow to breast the waves. In Kerry the same boat also survives.

The Welsh have a much better-recorded tradition of seafaring than the Irish. It is surprising, though, how closely their maritime legends parallel those of the Irish. They sailed the waters round Iceland before the Vikings; they were credited with discovering magical islands; they even had their American discovery myth. This held that twelfth-century Prince Madoc had been there 300 years before Columbus. It was a particularly powerful myth. It led to the belief that somewhere in America was a lost tribe of white Indians who were Welsh-speaking descendants of Prince Madoc and his crew. It was revived in the fifteenth century by the English to counter the Spanish claims to exclusive ownership of the Americas. If British people had been there in the twelfth century, how could such a claim be exclusive?

From then on, Madoc was a recurrent phenomenon in the exploitation of America. Two
Welshmen, John Evans and Morgan John Rhys,
charted a large section of the Missouri basin in the
search for their long-lost brothers. When they
finally came upon the 'Mandans', as these Indians
were known, they had to admit that there was not
one phrase of Welsh among them. Still, the myth
stimulated a flood of emigrants across the Atlantic
and gave the Welsh a pride in their seafaring
abilities.

The strangest thing I experienced in Wales was
neither myth nor museum artefact. It was a custom
called 'Cymanfaoedd Pwync' which consisted of
musical chanting the likes of which I had not heard
before or since. It took place in a small chapel in a
village called Maenchlochog Dhu, meaning the
Black Monk's Bell. The entire congregation assembled in the body of the chapel, divided itself into
four sections, two male and two female and,
without benefit of a conductor, launched into a
fierce and startling recital. The music was as far
from any European form as the sean-nōs singing of
my own locality. Not that it resembled sean-nōs; it
was the exact opposite: like a war chant, loud and
staccato. Each musical phrase was the same,
simply two notes repeated for as long as the words
required. I was surprised to discover they were
reading, in Welsh, from the Bible.

These people, worshipping in a perfectly normal
way, appeared to have retained the uninhibited
fundamentalism that must have imbued early
Christianity. Explanations as to the origin of the
chant were, as usual, vague. There was the prosaic
explanation that this was a technique used by old
missionaries to instill by rote the words of the
gospel into the heads of children. The parents, as
so often happens, learned from the children. Just
as mathematical tables were once learned off by

heart, without much comprehension, so the object was to imprint the words indelibly on people's minds.

It is just as likely that the chant was pre-missionary, part of the secular culture of the people; could it have been, like so many other things, absorbed into the Christian form of worship? I have heard of preachers in the south of Wales who could work themselves up into such a frenzy of oratory that it became almost a musical recital. The BBC once recorded them, intercut the sound with that of a muezzin, and dared anyone to tell them apart. It was reminiscent of that occasion, a century before in the Royal Irish Academy, when the man from Lebanon and the Irish antiquarian also exchanged notes.

The day after this recital I was inspecting a large megalithic structure called Pentre Ifan. It was similar to those I had seen all over Ireland, in Brittany, right down the Atlantic coasts to Galicia. Following the cartographical lesson of E.G. Bowen, I made a mental note that all of the chapels and Sunday schools in which Cymanfaoedd Pwync is sung are on the same Welsh peninsula that contains St David's Cathedral as well as the Cilgerran coracle. This is the peninsula that reaches furthest out towards the Atlantic. It is called Dyfed.

At this stage, I discovered a study that suggested the sought-after links might be more than cultural: a survey by A.E. Mourant and I. Morgan Watkin of the blood groups, anthropology and language in Wales and western countries. Mourant and Watkin found that the peoples of the peripheral north-western regions of Europe – Iceland, Scotland, Ireland and parts of Wales – showed A, B and O blood groups with a frequency almost identical with the Sardinians, the Cretans and certain Berber tribes of North Africa. This does not prove that these people are the same, or are even descended from the same ancestor: the similarity could be due to the coincidental effects of inter-marriage and isolation. The theory that, beyond cultural links, there might be a racial link, a migration in pre-history, is too obscured by time to be certain. But more solid evidence was to be found in Western megalithic culture.

Down the Atlantic coasts of Europe the mega-liths (literally, 'big stones') reach like gigantic stepping stones. They link places as far apart as Denmark, Scotland, Galicia and southern Spain. They are the dolmens, menhirs, passage graves, some of them immense in construction, which stand as permanent testimony to the imagination and organization of a race or races who were essentially seafarers. The passage graves of New-grange, Knowth and Dowth in Co Meath, with their massive scale, strange carvings and astrono-mical precision are exactly counterpointed by those in Morbihan on the coast of Brittany. The designs are quite similar, the layouts identical, the location near water – a river in one case, the sea in another – all point to an undeniable relationship. There can be no doubt that the people who built them were in direct maritime contact.

These megaliths are the most solid evidence that as far back as 3000 BC, before the pyramids of Egypt were built, man carried his culture up and down the Atlantic coasts. Despite many local variations the passage graves in Maes Howe, Orkney, share the same tradition as those in Alcala, Portugal, or Huelva, Spain. They profound-ly undermine the standard idea of cultural spread happening primarily overland.

Evidence has been produced to suggest that the megaliths of the northern areas, in fact, predate their counterparts in the south. The relationship to Minos and Mycenae is here invoked. Undoutedly, there is a clear similarity between the layout and designs of these eastern Mediterranean structures and those of the Atlantic areas. The entrances to the Palace of Minos on Crete and the Newgrange passage grave are remarkably alike. But the dispute over chronology, which came first, tends to obscure the main point. It is a red herring in front of the fact that the Mediterranean and the Atlantic expressions of this culture are related directly. Gordon Childe made a direct analogy, in reverse, when he suggested that we should notice that the areas on which the Vikings made an impression are the same as those in which the megalithic forms appear. If the Vikings could have such a wide influence, why not imagine an earlier race doing the same thing?

The problem seems to be a lack of confidence in the idea that Neolithic man was technologically equipped to sail long distances. This, despite the fact that all scholars now agree that the sea was an easier and safer form of travel when the land was forested and filled with wild animals. Thor Heyerdahl always insisted that man hoisted a sail before he saddled a horse. All the evidence shows that even when early man penetrated inland, he clung very closely to the waterways.

The seagoing capacity of our Stone Age forebears is greatly underestimated. Marine archaeology is still in its infancy. Water covers seven-eighths of the planet and is still encroaching, in some areas, at the rate of an inch a year. If this rate has been constant over the past 5000 years the remnants of coastal dwellings of centuries ago must all be covered by water. In order to get a truer picture of the movements of people in the past it may be necessary for archaeologists to don snorkels.

The builders of the megaliths would have used wood for their boats. It is unlikely that remains would survive on the seabed, waiting for us to discover them. The oldest remains that have so far been discovered in our northern areas are dug-out canoes made from single trees and preserved in bogs. But Thor Heyerdahl has demonstrated that these are not necessarily the earliest form of marine craft. The ancient Assyrians – admittedly later than the megalith builders – were able to carry a complete chariot together with a crew of possibly twenty people in their 'quffas', the large equivalent of the coracle. If they could do this with skin-covered vessels, what could others have fashioned from wood? Sea boats usually end up on rocks or beaches if they are not sunk further out. The chances of even a single wooden wreck lasting through centuries of the kinds of storms we have on the Atlantic coasts are very unlikely.

The mysteries of the megaliths will never be solved until they are approached from a more open perspective than that of the landlubber. They are a problem which will not be resolved until archaeology becomes as efficient on the sea as on the land. But, at this stage of my quest, it did not seem too much to maintain that, quite independently of central Europe, the peoples of these Atlantic coasts were in direct maritime contact as long ago as 5000 years, and that this contact extended from Scandinavia to the Mediterranean.

# chapter six

I visited all the oceans, I saw the
    misty West,
There, where clouds are born,
    and beauty.
I saw Medina and also Mecca,
    and Egypt and Jerusalem.
In Sudan I watched the great
    rivers.
From the top of the plateau I
    saw the world.
Take my advice friend, dis-
    mount here;
No place is lovelier than Amur.

Amur is an old Berber name for Morocco. I came across the poem in a magazine published in Rabat which was devoted to reviving the Berber language and culture. I was fascinated by this magazine because its arguments seemed to reproduce all the sentiments of the Irish language revival of eighty years ago. There was a difference, however slight, in that it appeared to me to be unlikely that the Berber culture and language could ever be indissolubly bound to the religion of Islam. The fortunes of the Irish language became linked to Catholicism, a development that ultimately, in my opinion, has worked against the existence of the language.

However, Berber revivalism is not quite the proper way to describe the philosophy of this magazine; its object was to achieve formal acknowledgement that the Berber languages and cultures were central to the identities of Morocco, Algeria and the other countries of North Africa. The official language is Arabic, and French is widely spoken: Morocco was a French colony for a century. Morocco is the only North African country that was not also dominated by the Turks which meant one less cultural layer to peel away and discover the heart of the country.

In a quiet street near the Grand Mosque in Rabat, I came across the Louis Chatelain archaeological museum. The museum was mainly devoted to the glories of Greece and Rome which, predictably, I ignored. But there was also a fine collection of Phoenician coins which whetted my interest. What I was looking for would not be prominent: it could be a coin, a map, a design, anything with a 'Celtic' echo – a category in which I still vaguely believed as some kind of reference point.

There were plenty of old stones, some with delicate carvings of animals, a reminder that the Sahara was once a green and fertile place, supporting a large population. Others had inscriptions in Libyan/Berber which indicated that these people have been literate at least as long as the residents of the British Isles.

A display of Roman metalwork showed designs to which I could easily attribute an Irish likeness. One in particular – a piece of harness – was fashioned as a triskele, a favourite detail of Irish art. However, this was explained away by the possibility of the Roman armies including 'Celtic' tradesmen in their number. In fact, the triskele is simply a variation of one of the most ancient and universal symbols, the swastika. The running legs of the Isle of Man is the example nearest home. There were certainly 'Britons' in the Roman army; whether as soldiers or as tradesmen, or victims of the press gang, nobody knows. In Volubilis, a figure of a man is shown wearing plaid trousers and the inscription identifies him as a 'Briton' although it was the Irish (Scotti) who originally used this garb. In the area of the desert called the Fayoum in Egypt, a sword was found, dated to the third century and described as 'Celtic'.

A single stone, called the Stele Maaziz, tucked away in the corner of the museum, caught my eye. It was approximately three feet high and featured a carved figure of indeterminate sex surrounded by a snaky, wavy line and, outside that, a series of overlapping concentric half-circles. The arrangement of these circles reminded me of the entrance stone to Newgrange as well as designs on the kerb-stones in the vicinity. I had also seen the snake-like line on stones in Ireland; here I learned that it could be traced back to Egypt and symbolized a serpent protecting the Sun God in his tomb – a good way of describing the winter solstice. This, of course, is the principal feature of the tumulus at Newgrange, where on 21 December, the rising sun penetrates a passage which is sixty-two feet in length, and then illuminates a central inner chamber.

The wavy and concentric designs were common on stones in strange places with strange names like Oukaimeden, Aougdal and n'Ouagouns – all Berber.

The French scholar George Souville wrote that they could not be accurately dated; however, to my delight, he pronounced the following: 'These different sorts of decorations are well-known on numerous monuments, stelae or engravings on the Atlantic coast from Ireland to Portugal, from Brittany to Galicia. The serpent-like motif appears on the menhirs from Minio in Brittany and reappears in Portugal and Spain. Concentric circles and semi-circles are motifs very widespread in Ireland, on Breton megaliths, notably at Gavr'inis, also in Galicia and Portugal.' George Souville linked these stones with the Bronze Age and, more particularly, with what he referred to as the

'Civilization of the Bronze-Atlantic'.

Before I left the Louis Chatelain museum, a French lady curator told me of a stone-circled tumulus in a place called M'Zora which was much further north, near Tangier. She even produced a faded photograph of the place. It was sufficiently intriguing for me to resolve to visit it. In the town of Larache, I was directed inland to a small town called Sidi Yemani. Its main street consisted of brown mud, churned up by the rain and looking like something out of an Alaskan gold rush. A young passer-by looked amused at my pidgin French as I tried to describe a tumulus and a circle of standing stones. 'Ah,' he said in perfect English, 'you mean the cromlech. Come, I shall take you there.'

I drove the hired car for two miles on a track carved out by a stream. Due to the rain, the stream had now reasserted its authority. It was the busy pathway between Sidi Yemani and the village where, I was informed, the cromlech stood. Eventually, we had to abandon the car and start hiking. It took another two miles of squelching through the mud to reach the site. It was set in the middle of a cluster of houses and gardens. The last time I saw an identical stone was at Punchestown, in Naas, Co Kildare. Coming nearer, we could see the circle of stones, some of them trespassing on gardens. It was true. It was the remains of a tumulus. Most of the central part had been gouged out, probably for the stones and gravel, just as similar tombs had been in Ireland. Many of these houses were probably built from the material. There were 167 stones in the circle according to our count. The pillar dominated the landscape. Newgrange once boasted such a stone. It was last seen in 1770.

The guide told me there was a reconstruction of the tumulus in a museum in Tetuan, seventy kilometres away. There, the following morning, after much bureaucratic difficulty – I had, after all, no academic credentials and no written permissions, so necessary in Morocco – I managed to take two pictures of what was, to me, unmistakably a first cousin of Newgrange and Gavr'inis. I learned that the site had been mentioned by a Roman historian, Sertorius. It was also described as being the grave of a native god, Antee; this coincided with the tradition of Newgrange being the grave of an Irish pagan god, Aonghus.

What was disturbing was to have to go to so much trouble to learn about a prominent landmark with which many archaeologists must be familiar. Among British and Irish archaeologists, the only reference to North African neolithic constructions I could find was from Glyn Daniel in his *Megalith Builders of Western Europe*. There was reference to menhirs in Algeria which are simple standing stones and which were defined as much later than those on the Atlantic coasts. There was no reference that I could find to the tumulus of M'Zora, the strongest evidence of connections. Certainly, French and Spanish archaeologists knew about it – the French and Spanish were, of course, the colonizers of Morocco – and an American, James W. Mavor, had written about *The Riddle of M'zorah*.

The most acceptable explanation I got for the relationship between Newgrange and M'Zora was contained in the word: polygenesis. This suggests that people with absolutely no cultural contact can easily develop habits of life, forms of worship and burial which are similar. They might discover fire, invent the wheel at the same time and without the slightest idea of each other's existence. It was not beyond the bounds of possibility that Neolithic man in Morocco developed the forms of the passage grave, the tumulus crowned with a phallic-shaped stone and surrounded by shaped

73

stones, quite independently of the 'farmers' on the Boyne 5000 years ago. Even the designs on the Stele Maaziz could be explained away. The spiral and circle are universal symbols, used in places as far apart as China and America. The spiral, for instance, is always 'at hand' as you can see by studying your fingerprints. Even the Japanese built what could be called 'megaliths'.

I was urged to consider the modern phenomenon of two physicists working at opposite sides of the globe; they can quite 'independently' come up with the solution to an intricate problem.

However, two physicists today, no matter how geographically separated, are by virtue of their discipline working in precisely the same intellectual environment, have access to the same references and precedents; belong, in fact, to a very specific scientific community. As Arthur Koestler pointed out, Leibnitz and Newton developed the infinitesimal calculus apparently independently, but they shared a long line of precursors. If Neolithic people of North Africa hit upon the same method of burying their dead, or erecting monuments, and used the same designs as other peoples on the Atlantic coasts, what 'long line of precursors' did they share?

It seemed, to me, that polygenesis or isolationism and its opposite – diffusion, meaning cultural spread – are theories which seem to be used selectively. If one sees similarities between the British Isles and North Africa, that is called polygenesis or coincidence. However, in the matter of Hallstatt or La Tene in Central Europe, as compared to the British Isles, that is accepted as diffusion or direct cultural contact.

It is quite respectable to see a solid neolithic connection between the Aryan – or even pre-Aryan – races of Scandinavia and the British Isles; one can even see connections with Crete – comfortably part of Mediterranean Europe. But it is going a little far to include what are thought to be the dark-skinned people of North Africa.

In fact, as I had already learned, the Berbers are not remotely what one could call dark-skinned and I, myself, am as sallow-complexioned as some Arabs I have met. Some Berber communities who keep to themselves and have maintained a traditional life-style boast a complexion lighter than some of my neighbours. They live mainly in the smaller towns of Morocco and on market day are easily distinguishable: the older women have tattoo marks on their faces. Most have a simple, inconspicuous mark on their foreheads but I saw women whose entire face and hands were covered with a complex tracery of designs. These patterns were consistent with the decoration on pottery and carpets, for which the Berbers are famous and which, for subtlety of composition, are hard to match.

The Berber males were traditionally the shock troops of the various conquerors, having the same problem as the Irish; an inability to pool their various tribal resources and collectively repel invaders. Still, their horsemanship is renowned and annually celebrated in summer festivals. A line of horsemen gallop furiously across an open space and suddenly, without any evident signal, loose their rifles at the same moment as they halt their gallop. Then they turn and repeat the exercise endlessly. This is called the Fantasie but its origins are far from fantasy. Whenever the Berbers could combine forces, they formed impressive dynasties like the Almoravids and the Almohads. These swept across Morocco and spread throughout Algeria, Tunisia and Libya. In the eleventh century they came to the rescue of the Muslim rulers of Spain who were threatened by Christian forces.

The French colonists in the nineteenth century

were able successfully to manipulate the distinction between Berber and Arab on the principle of divide and conquer. The tension is still echoed today; those who are aware of this period will say: we are neither Arab nor Berber; we are Moroccans. As successive historians have pointed out, the invasions of North Africa by Phoenicians, Greeks, Romans, Byzantines, Vandals, Arabs and Turks probably constituted small ruling élites, technologically superior but, in the main, transient. Thus, the ethnic characteristics of the indigenous population, the Berbers, may have remained substantially the same.

The Berbers themselves produced a succession of leaders like Massinissa, Jugurtha, Juba etc. These variously opposed and collaborated with the invaders according to the political expedients of the time. Their successors demonstrated this independence of mind in religious affairs: when Rome was pagan, the Berbers adopted Christianity and Judaism; when Rome became Christian they adopted the 'heretical' Arianism. They adopted Islam against the Byzantines but when Islam became oppressive they developed their own liberal forms of that religion. Again, when Muslim rulers developed decadent tendencies, the Berbers overthrew them and reasserted a puritan regime.

I learned that certain eminent figures of the Roman Church were of North African and Berber origin. Even St Augustine was an Algerian. Tertullian, a celebrated Father of the Church before he reverted to 'heresy', seems to have been an early pacifist. He recognized only one nation, 'that which has no border but the universe' and only one republic, 'the world'. He denied Christians the right to join any army or institution of the state – hence his falling out with Rome, I suppose. He seems to have been the first prominent preacher of the idea of conscientious objection.

Pope Paul VI in his 1967 message to the Africans, recognized the significance of these early Berber Christians. He acknowledged that 'from the second to the fourth centuries AD, there was very intense Christian life in the Northern regions of Africa'. In the domain of theology, North Africa was very much to the fore. From my childhood I remembered the names Origen (who also became 'heretical'), Cyril, St Cyprian, Athanasius, Tertullian, Augustine being droned out in the litanies of Sunday Mass. It was a slight shock to find that these were all North Africans.

The Berber who most intrigued me came later. He was Ibn Khaldoun, who lived in the fourteenth century. When I came across the name Averroes, the Father of Sociology, I assumed he was a Latin-speaking European. He turned out to be Moroccan. He wrote:

Historians ... have committed frequent errors in the stories and events they reported. They accepted them in plain transmitted form, without regard for its value. They did not probe them with the yardstick of philosophy, with the help of the knowledge of the nature of things, or with the help of speculation and historical insight. Therefore they strayed from the truth and found themselves lost in the desert of baseless assumptions and errors.

I travelled to Meknes, Fez, Marrakech and many places in between, always looking for details but inevitably taking in the magnificence of Islamic civilization. The scale of the architecture of mosques and palaces was beyond petty human pride. The old imperial palace of Meknes, for instance, was so large one needed a taxi to cover the extensive grounds. But the intricate detail, the sheer brilliance of the decoration of each door and window was awesome. A single clear religious belief was the driving force.

The unselfconsciousness with which people removed their shoes on entering the Karaouine Mosque in Fez, rolled up their sleeves and washed themselves before prostrating themselves in prayer became, for me, not a slightly ludicrous activity but evidence of an inevitable sureness of identity. I thought sadly of the bored, dutiful approach of Westerners to church on Sundays. No wonder Islam cut like a sword through the dissipation of Christendom so many centuries ago.

In a museum of Berber art in Meknes, the curator directed me to objects which she herself felt had an affinity with 'Celtic' art. This led me on to the Berber jewellery which was astonishing in its sophistication. It consisted of elaborate head-dresses, necklets and bracelets which I was informed were the Berber 'bank'. All of the family's wealth, in the form of coins or precious metals, was incorporated in female adornments. Thus, if two families were contemplating a liaison, they could each tell at a glance the potential for a dowry. From the dates on the coins it was clear that although this was an old custom, it had the distinction of still being practised. It was as if the ancient gold lunulae in the National Museum in Dublin were still being made and sported by the Irish.

The construction of the jewellery and the tiny designs on it struck a chord with me: the Tara Brooch.

I took the precaution of not relying on my own impressions. Back in Ireland, I asked a sculptress friend to comment. Cliodna Cussen immediately saw the resemblance, went so far as to name the Tara Brooch and felt sure that, if one looked hard enough through samples of Irish art, one would find at least one of the designs, a distinct four-sided version of the 'triskele'. She made the point that, in general, the feeling of the jewellery was oriental but that, in the detail, there were certainly echoes of Irish art. This applied particularly, she said, to the Berber habit of filling every crevice with a design. The 'Celts', she said, shared this 'horror vacui'.

Everything unusual or distinctive about Ireland seemed to be, consciously or unconsciously, lumped into the vague category 'Celtic'. The 'Celts' were becoming, for me, a historical cul-de-sac beyond which investigation was almost pointless. It was bad enough that all of the most interesting things about Ireland should be explained away – and thus not truly explained – by reference to some obscure central European race. But it seemed that this obfuscation had already been applied to the Berbers.

A report from the *Caledonian Medical Journal* of 1908 had the striking title: 'Celtic Tribes in Morocco'. Dr George Mackey of Edinburgh stated that 'he had learned from a military friend who had made more than one expedition into Morocco that there was reason to believe that there existed there at the present time a race of people of Celtic origin'.

I read on – the article detailed the various cultural elements that made up the population of the country, and then continued:

> There is a fourth and extremely interesting race that is neither Arab nor Jew and that speaks a language having no connection with either. This is the race to which the wild, warlike Berber tribes belong, who inhabit the mountains and table-lands of the interior. They owe allegiance to no-one and although nominally Mohammedan do not practise

polygamy. The Sultan does not venture to pass through their territory and actually pays toll to some of them in order to be allowed along their frontiers without being molested on his way from Fez to Morocco [*sic*].

But to speakers of Gaelic the most interesting fact connected with the Berber tribes is that they speak a language called Shloh or Shluh, which a Gaelic-speaking medical missionary, who had travelled amongst them in the Atlas mountains and Sus country, told me he at once recognized as Celtic.

Although he had no previous knowledge of it and had no conception of its being allied to Gaelic, he found himself able to understand much of what was being said the first time he went among the tribes solely on account of the resemblance of their language to his own Gaelic.

The best known have names that closely resemble the clan names of MacTier, MacDougall and MacGhill, namely the famous Berber clans of the M'Tir, the M'Tuga and the M'Ghill, to give them their Arabic spelling. The Arabs speak of them as the Bini M'Tir, but the Bini which is Arabic for children is a reduplication of the Shloh or Gaelic 'M' or 'Mac', having the same meaning.

Dr Mackey added that the Berbers were widely distributed and were essentially mountaineers which was the main reason they were able to maintain their independence. He also claimed that the facial type of the Berbers was said to resemble the 'black celt of Scotland', unmixed with Scandinavian stock. 'It did not appear,' he said, 'that they had any literature but they had bagpipes.'

I have met Breton musicians who are convinced that the Kabyle music of Algeria is identical to their own and they all use bagpipes, the national instrument of Scotland. The Irish, too, have their own bagpipes called the uilleann pipes.

Although respectable scholarship regularly assigns such articles to what they call the 'lunatic fringe' of academe, it is extraordinary how persistent are the attempts to explain that which standard scholarship cannot: in this case, certain unusual aspects of both North Africa and the British Isles. The 'Celtic' categorization might be irritating to me but at least it admitted affinity between the two areas. There have been, down the years, numerous references such as the above published. In the *Dublin Penny Journal* of 1834 the following appeared:

> About the close of the last century, a gentleman who was superintending the digging out of potatoes in the county of Antrim (Northern Ireland), was surprised to see some sailors who had entered the field, in conversation with his labourers, who only spoke Irish. He went to them and learned that the sailors were from Tunis and that the vessel to which they belonged had put into port from stress of weather. The sailors and country people understood each other, the former speaking the language used at Tunis, and the latter speaking Irish. This anecdote was related by a person of credit and must interest the Irish scholar.

This episode would have occurred at the end of the eighteenth century when the Barbary corsairs were still active, so the presence of a ship from Tunis is quite believable. Whether intelligent discourse took place is a matter for the degree of one's scepticism.

Another incident was reported by a J.S. Buckingham, a member of the Syro-Egyptian Society, meeting in the London Athenaeum in 1845. He declared that a few years previously, in Dorchester, he had met a 'native of Morocco, whose name was Saadi Ombeck Benbei'. The merchant stated, in the presence of Mr and Mrs Buckingham, that he had visited Ireland and stayed at Kilkenny where:

> he went one day to the post office and hearing there for the first time some of the labouring people speaking Irish, he was surprised to find he could understand their conversation; as the language had a strong resemblance to the dialect of the mountaineers of Mount Atlas, in Africa, among whom he had travelled and traded in his youth and learned their language. He addressed the labourers in this language and their surprise was as great as his own to find they understood him. The dialogue was very short and on ordinary topics; but he declared there was not any difficulty in understanding each other.

Mr Buckingham went on to talk about a woman who had originally come from the west of Ireland, spoke Gaelic fluently and married a consul to a port in Morocco – which Buckingham thought was near Mogador; that 'she was surprised to find herself able to converse with the mountaineers of the country who brought in the poultry, vegetables and fruit to the market for sale'.

There were other independent references to all the above incidents. One of these came from Lieutenant-Colonel Chesney's account of his 'Expedition to the Euphrates and Tigris', published in 1850. Another source was Edward Clibborn, curator of the Royal Irish Academy in 1859, who was not entirely dismissive when he also recounted the stories. He even quoted the opinion of a well-known Irish antiquarian, Eugene O'Curry – a Gaelic speaker – who said: 'He would not be at all astonished to learn that the Irish language was still in existence in Northern Africa.' However, O'Curry attributed the possibility to the number of Irish captives brought there by the Barbary corsairs.

Clibborn mentioned several other pieces of evidence:

> The fact of a discovery of the wreck of a very ancient ship on the coast of Wexford, containing two chambered cannons, made of bars of hooped iron, and said to be exactly of the same manufacture as that of guns fished up in the harbour of Constantinople, and the same as old pieces of ordnance found on the walls of Canton, tends to raise the possibility that African pirates or traders or both of them, did visit the coast as early as the reign of Edward III and possibly before the time of the Danes, whose visits to the Mediterranean may possibly have been intended to keep in check the corsairs, and cover their own piracies in the open seas.

Mr Clibborn was described to me by a Dublin archaeologist as a very unreliable and unmethodical observer; further, cannons made of bars of iron were a very common mediaeval form of construction. Clibborn, who was the curator of the Royal Irish Academy, was himself fairly sceptical of the Gaelic in North Africa theory. Nevertheless, he wrote:

> I confess I think there must be some truth at the bottom of the old tradition which brings the 'Milesian' population of Ireland from Getulia in Northern Africa notwithstanding that ethnologists claim the language of Ireland

as belonging to the Japhetic class of languages. But if Japhetic, its elementary sounds appear to be more African than European, for an educated African can read Irish manuscript with perfect accuracy as to the sounds of the letters; and thus a good ear, listening to people speaking rapidly both Irish and Arabic, or that had heard one language here and the other in Morocco, being ignorant of both, might readily assume the languages to be identical, the radical sounds being the same.

The man who compiled a number of these stories and opinions in the last century was Robert MacAdam. He seemed to take seriously the old legends of Irish origins, too, despite the fact that many scholars cast aspersions on them and describe them as monkish inventions. MacAdam summarized his researches thus:

The old and circumstantial account of a colony established in Ireland from Spain takes us a long way on the Road to North Africa; and if true would render it very possible that the colonists or their ancestors came previously from that country to Spain. In such case it would not be at all impossible that some tribe of the same race may have remained and settled in the present Morocco or Tunis and have been eventually driven to the mountains at the time of the destruction of Carthage or subsequently by the overwhelming pressure of the Moors.

Speculation however is useless until we obtain more definite information regarding the supposed cognate language existing in that country; and the object of the present article is merely to place the preceding facts together on record and to direct the attention of competent inquirers to a curious subject.

# chapter seven

Scholarly opinion is now inclined to dismiss reports that Irish Gaelic speakers could converse with Berbers: a Celtic scholar from Switzerland was correct when he said to me that it was 'very unlikely' that I might understand Berber. Nevertheless, Professor Wagner represents a school of linguistics which maintains that underneath Gaelic, Welsh and the other 'insular Celtic' languages, exercising a formative influence on them and still clearly detectable, there lies another language or languages which they identify as Hamito-Semitic, ie of the Middle East and North Africa.

The model of one language replacing another and retaining traces of the first is fairly straightforward. English is now the principal language of Ireland, having slowly replaced Gaelic over the past three centuries. Conamara is one of the few places left where people conduct their business in Gaelic. When you hear an Irish person saying 'I'm after being in hospital', it is not an indication of bizarre thought processes but a direct translation from the Gaelic: 'Tá mē tharēis bheith 'san ospuidēal'. The syntax of Gaelic still survives in the speech of many Irish people despite years of English-language schooling and, more recently, exposure to the dialect of American soap operas.

This half-life of Gaelic in English-speaking people can be described as a linguistic substratum. Now, logically, if the English as spoken in Ireland has a Gaelic substratum, then Gaelic, if and when it first spread over the island 2500 years ago, must have equally been influenced by whatever language was previously *in situ*. This substratum was claimed by Professor Wagner and his colleagues to have distinct typological affinities with Berber, Egyptian, Arabic and Hebrew.

This area of linguistic research was initiated as far back as 1899 by Welsh scholar Morris Jones; it was further developed by Julius Pokorny who in turn taught Heinrich Wagner. Wagner came to Ireland in 1946 from Switzerland where, along with Gaelic, he had studied Arabic and Hebrew. The first thing he did was look up Morris Jones' article in the library of the Dublin Institute for Advanced Studies. To his surprise, he found that the pages of the book were uncut, which meant that nobody had read the article. A colleague of his, David Greene – another eminent Celtic scholar – told him that students were discouraged from reading it on the grounds that it was irrelevant and slightly mad. As Wagner pointed out to me, Sir Morris Jones was one of the most respected Welsh scholars. According to the professor, such an idea did not suit the cultural and philosophic ethos that prevailed in the early years of this century.

Unfortunately, when dealing with languages spoken thousands of years ago, practically nothing is known with certainty. All is speculation; the very existence of 'Celtic' or 'Indo-European' as languages cannot be demonstrated, only deduced. As Professor David Greene put it, it is 'as if all the records of Latin had been wiped out and we set out to reconstruct it from the speech of French, Italians, Spaniards and Rumanians of today'.

This area – linguistic analysis – was the most difficult and tortuous I had yet encountered. The term 'Indo-European' is simply a description of the earliest recognizable stage in the development of one group of the languages of the world. It does not, contrary to popular belief, refer to a race of people. David Greene summed it up well: 'To say that the Greeks or Hindus were Indo-Europeans is like saying that the French or Rumanians are ancient Romans; their languages may be lineal descendants of that of the ancient Romans, but that is a different matter.'

The term 'Celtic' is as theoretical as 'Indo-European'. Neither term has any ethnic significance and neither should be used to describe a particular culture.

Wagner's opponents were described by him as neo-grammarians and 'structuralists'. They held the view that language developed according to the workings of mechanical and psychological laws, known as the 'sound laws' and the 'laws of analogy'. They tend to overlook the influence of social history on the development of language. This suggested to me that if people develop their language 'mechanically', they do it without reference to their neighbours. The ultimate of this would be a baby learning to talk without listening to its parents.

Some scholars would confine examination of matters 'Celtic' to Europe and points east, would rely on a postulated movement of such a language from central Europe out to the fringes – a parallel to what Dr Joseph Raftery has dismissed as the 'Thomas Cook school of archaeology'. This school would admit possible links with Sanscrit and, in particular, Hittite – all safely within the definition of Aryan. But extend the area of study in a southerly direction – to the Middle East proper and North Africa – and the shutters come down. For instance, ten years after Morris Jones published his ideas two other major works appeared: a comparative Celtic grammar by Pedersen (pupil of Brugmann, father of neo-grammarianism) and an *Old Irish Grammar* by Thurneysen. Both works ignored Morris Jones' findings.

As Heinrich Wagner put it: 'Whenever it can be

proved by scholars who do not adhere to the teaching of any rigid school, that a dying language has influenced considerably the growth and development of the language by which it is superseded, the neo-grammarians use the term "substratum theory", as if the recognition of substratum influence were based on "theory" alone and not on observations in the field.'

'We are here,' he says, 'dealing with a sociolinguistic fact of the highest historical importance.' Heinrich Wagner had travelled and worked in Ireland, Wales and the Isle of Man, Brittany, Lapland, Finland, the Basque country, learning the languages and studying them in detail. His linguistic atlas of Ireland is a standard work.

Essentially, what he was saying was that if in the British Isles, at some dim and distant time, a language loosely called 'Celtic' had been imposed on a people who were 'non-Celtic', then the latter – the indigenous inhabitants – must have spoken a language or languages unknown and that this must have strongly influenced the development of the new language. The basic observation behind this insight was that many features of this new 'insular-Celtic' language had no parallels in other Indo-European languages. In other words, there were aspects of Gaelic which were not paralleled in, say, French or English.

Further, by using a kind of linguistic archaeology, Professor Wagner had delved through the intervening layers and found features in 'insular Celtic' which had affinities with, for instance, Egyptian – the language of the Copts – and Berber. These oddities, which appeared consistently in Gaelic, included the position of the verb at the beginning of the sentence – a feature which is not typical of Indo-European and modern European languages. There was a further similarity that Berber 'suffixes or infixes pronominal objects', according to Wagner, in a way that is, in principle, identical to the rules governing the use of the old Irish verb.

The language which he suggested existed before Gaelic also shared some of the affinities with Basque, which everybody agrees is not of Indo-European origin. Although most scholars believe that Basque is loosely related to Caucasian, nobody can explain the existence of this people or how they arrived at the Pyrenees. It was suggested that the Picts of Scotland also spoke a non-Indo-European language. When Gaelic-speaking missionaries of the early Middle Ages went to convert them they had to use interpreters. It is also on record that Cormac, an Irish king of the ninth century, described the language of the people of Munster, in the south-west of Ireland, as the 'iron language', presumably because it was unintelligible to him, a Gaelic speaker.

Most scholars would agree that the terms 'Celtic' and 'Indo-European' were purely theoretical and had, or should have, no racial interpretation. Yet, these terms are still used as descriptions of actual races of peoples. Many books have been written about the 'Celts'. Some admit, initially, that the term should not be used in an ethnic sense; all proceed to do precisely this.

Herodotus contains the first recorded use of the term. He made a casual reference to people living on the Danube. The Greeks followed suit with the term 'Keltoi' and added the term 'Galatae'. The Romans then continued the process and defined the Gauls. These terms were used with considerable looseness and there is not any serious evidence that any of these peoples described themselves as 'Celts'. A writer named Poseidonius seems to have been the first Greek to use the term 'Keltoi'. He thought Europeans were divided equally into Scythians and Celts. He didn't apparently realize that Northern Europeans were divided into many different tribes and peoples – just as they are today. In fact, his opinions are only known to us through quotations from Cicero, Livy, Marcellinus, Virgil, Lucan and Italicus. They all got their information from this one writer and his words only exist in their quotations.

As far as the Irish acceptance of the title 'Celt' is concerned, my friend Desmond Fennell has put it well: 'I think we should leave this usage of "Celtic" to foreigners; partly because the description of Irish mental processes as "Celtic" has been an instrument of colonization.'

The more I investigated the 'Celtic' world, the less it became a reliable means of identifying the Irish, Welsh, Scottish etc. The whole intellectual construct resembled a house of cards. A prominent archaeologist, Liam de Paor, wrote: 'Apart from language, what they (Irish, Welsh, Scots etc) have in common that we might identify as "Celtic" is largely artificial and the result of romantic or nationalist revivalism of the past two or three centuries.'

There is no evidence which would justify us speaking of Celtic Art – or even Celtic Literature. As Robin Flower put it:

Another and more insidious enemy of our subject is the popular and general use of the word 'Celtic' in literary criticism. Irish literature may be properly described as 'Celtic', if we are to understand by that simply that it is the product of a people speaking a Celtic language. But the word is commonly taken to mean much more than that . . . vagueness and mist and an indefinite use of dubiously poetic language has been generally held to be the undubitable mark of Celticism.

In Ireland, the entire 'Celtic' thesis rests on the belief that in approximately 500 BC, the island was invaded by a North European people who gave the island its language and culture. The Keeper of Irish Antiquities in the National Museum, Dublin, said to me that the material evidence for such a 'Celtic invasion' was slight. He added that the invasion thesis could, in the main, be regarded as 'wishful thinking'. An ex-director of the same museum, Dr Joseph Raftery, told me he was not at all convinced by what he described as 'this loose talk' of Celtic invasions. However, there is the Gaelic language which somebody must have brought to the island. Linguists have much more evidence than archaeologists.

If there was an invasion of such people it was most probably a tightly knit, numerically small group who, by virtue of their technological superiority, cut through the territories of the indigenous people on the island. The Anglo-Saxons did this in Britain. The Normans in the twelfth century are reputed to have had only 600 well-armed knights when they took over Ireland. The latter did not materially change the culture of the island; in fact, they ended up speaking Gaelic.

One of the ironies of the analogous 'Celtic' invasion is that much of the evidence, both material and literary, is found in the North of Ireland – a part of the island whose ruling ideology likes to distance itself from things 'Celtic'. Nevertheless, Celtic Irish mythology is largely constituted of what is called the Ulster Cycle, a series of epics which feature quarrels between Connacht and Ulster – between Queen Maeve and a Northern warrior, Setanta, sometimes known as Cuchulainn.

It is recorded in this epic that when Queen Maeve moved to attack Ulster she stood looking across the River Blackwater at 'the strange land'.

This perceived difference between Southern and Northern Ireland is one of the longest-running debates in Irish history. It even has a geological basis in that a line of drumlins runs like a barrier from Sligo to Carlingford Lough. A Southern scholar, P.L. Henry, has commented on these distinctions as 'one of the most deeply-rooted, ancient and – from a literary point of view – most productive facts of early history'.

Professor Henry complicated things a little further for me. He suggested that the Southern Irish were in a category called Q-Celts, from France, whereas the Northern Irish originated in Wales – hence the name Setanta – who were P-Celts and ultimately came from Iberia, ie Celt-Iberians. I was then brought full circle by Heinrich Wagner saying that the Iberian element of this relationship probably spoke a Hamitic, that is, Berber language.

The so-called 'Celtic' languages survive only on the western seaboard of Europe. They are believed to have come from the Continent – an idea based on place-names and inscriptions recorded mainly by Greeks and Romans. No Celtic language survives on the Continent. However, in material matters, the position is reversed. In continental Europe, there is much physical evidence to suggest a technologically well-developed people who had a mastery of bronze and iron-working. However, artefacts of identical design in Ireland are sparse. In fact, such artefacts as have been found on this island suggest more a continuity of design in Ireland than a sudden, dramatic change in the material culture. So it is really only on a linguistic basis that a migration from continental Europe is postulated, and a 'Celtic' identity attributed.

Is it inconceivable that the seafaring peoples of the western fringes of Europe could have developed a quite autonomous language and culture without depending on some imaginary central European race called 'Celts'? Is it not possible that the language spoken in these areas – the so-called 'insular Celtic' – was simply the language of these areas which had acquired a veneer of central European characteristics? After all, if the 'Celts' were such a mighty culture in Europe, was it likely the Romans would have erased all spoken trace of them? Eight hundred years after the Anglo-Norman invasion of Ireland, 300 years after the Tudor invasion, Gaelic is still spoken in Ireland. Were the Romans so much more efficient as to be able to wipe out completely the 'Celtic' language in Europe?

The Aran islands are the inhabited rocks off the west coast of Ireland which were immortalized in the writings of John Millington Synge, in the film *Man of Aran* by Robert O Flaherty and in the paintings of numerous artists. The islands are within a few miles of Conamara and are also Gaelic-speaking. Indeed, because of their extreme westerly position they are considered to be the last outpost of 'Celticism' by those subscribers to the aforementioned Thomas Cook school. If the Celtic invasion theory were true then these isolated and relatively unspoilt islanders should retain racial traces of the invaders.

Unfortunately for this romantic idea, the evidence does not bear it out. There is a major snag. The main blood group of the people of Aran is quite different, not only from that which is deemed to be 'Celtic' but from the bulk of the population of Ireland. The most fundamental badge of race is, here, not apparent. The anomaly can be explained by invasion, certainly; but it is a little more prosaic than the 'Celtic' scenario. In the seventeenth century, the western armies of Cromwell were garrisoned on the largest of the three islands. It appears these soldiers were almost forgotten and stayed long enough to make a considerable impact on the genes of the islanders. They also left their names. Even in Conamara there is a fairly wide sprinkling of the names of Windom, Grealish, Griffith, Welsh, Cook, Davy, Bolustrum. In passing – and in line with my general maritime orientation – it is worth noting how Cromwell chose an island to control the western areas; not for him a mainland stronghold – the various danger points were more accessible by sea.

It is surprising how pervasive the Celtic myth is when it is realized that many Irish scholars are quite sceptical of it. The myth certainly suited the politicians of the nineteenth and twentieth centuries and was rich material for Anglo-Irish poets. It was a means of defining – or perhaps creating – a national identity. It must have seemed a marvellous way of persuading a battered and demoralized people that they had a pedigree and potential impeccable enough to confront the British Empire. That the tactic worked is perhaps sufficient justification. There is little as powerful as an idea whose time has come.

By the same token, there is little as embarrassing as an obsolete idea which lingers on. There is some pragmatic justification for political animals to preserve the Celtic myth; when scholars subscribe to it, however sceptically or even inadvertently, there is cause for concern. As recently as 1981 a huge tome was published in Canada under the title *The Celtic Consciousness*. The object, ironically, was to provide a link and common background for French- and English-speaking Canadians. In fairness, the scholars who are sceptical about 'Celticism' but who, nevertheless, contributed to the book, were not responsible for the title. An indication of the book's 'scope' was the fact that a long article was included which detailed the prehistoric passage graves of the Atlantic regions – a phenomenon that pre-dated even the alleged arrival of the Celts by nearly 3000 years!

However, the works in the book were themselves excellent. A fine article by folklorist Kevin Danaher completely undermined a 'Celtic' basis for Irish folk tradition and culture. He pointed out that the traditional four-season year in Ireland was based entirely on solar reckoning, that in this tradition there was no time-reckoning by the moon and that the predominant element in Irish mythology was the sun. However, the Coligny calendar found in France, and attributed to the 'Celts', is lunar-based. Mr Danaher concluded that, in a number of important respects, the Irish tradition was not 'Celtic'. He went on to say: 'We cannot necessarily assume that because something is early Irish it is therefore Celtic'; and 'We might even go further and ask if we are not straining the bounds of scientific credibility by claiming that the Irish are a Celtic people.'

Other writers in *The Celtic Consciousness* echo this point. It might be considered to be Celtic cussedness to read, in such a book, that the Irish are not Celtic at all. But the demythologizing must start somewhere. It will be a long hard slog because the myth is all-pervasive. The most recent example I found was in my old friend John Arden's magnificent book *Silence among the Weapons*. In it a secondary character named Horsefury is described as a Celt. When he speaks there emerges a syntax which is unmistakably west of Ireland. The device is artistically clever and quite supportable. However, it is based on a classical understanding of 'Celticism' which I hope I have undermined.

If the Irish are not 'Celts' then, logically, neither are the Scots, Welsh, Manx, Bretons, Cornish or Galicians. So what are, who are, these people? If Liam de Paor is correct in describing the so-called

'Celtic' attributes as romantic inventions of the nineteenth century, then what are the links that undoubtedly bind these people into some kind of felt unity?

The peoples of the Atlantic seaways are isolated by modern communication systems: to visit each other they must travel uncomfortably by secondary routes. These areas form what has already been described as a cultural archipelago, having more in common with each other than with the centralized governments that control them – and have written their history.

It is difficult and unwieldy to describe these people, their culture and language without falling back on the vague, if convenient, title of 'Celts'. That is why I have opted for the term 'Atlantean'. At least it has some realistic maritime connotation and suggests a less jaded perspective from which to examine the subject. Logically, though, if the essence of this perspective is sea-based, then one must extend the catchment area further north to Iceland and western Scandinavia – areas which have admitted links with Ireland. But – and this is the hard part – it must also be extended southward, to those other people bordered by the Atlantic, the Moroccan Berbers.

The gap between Vallancey and Ledwich is, I hope, beginning to close.

# chapter eight

In the first century of Arab expansion, we hear of the Caliph, Abd El Malek, instructing his lieutenant in Africa to use Tunis as an arsenal and dockyard: from there they sailed out to conquer Sicily, Sardinia and Corsica. It did not take much seamanship to move across the few miles from Ceuta in Morocco to Gebal Tarik – Gibraltar – in 711 AD. Once they secured Spain, they could, at their leisure, investigate the Atlantic.

By the twelfth century the Arabs were the most advanced geographers. An Arab scholar who lived in Spain between 1002 and 1085 could comment on the whaling engaged in by ships off the west coast of Ireland. In the twelfth century, Al-Idrisi was the most prominent of these mediaeval specialists in geography. He also referred to the seafaring activities of the inhabitants of Ireland. It suggests that the people of this island must have been a little better equipped than those in the single example given by Giraldus Cambrensis: he referred to two semi-naked savages who paddled out in their canoe to meet the sailors on a British ship. They had never heard of Christ, never eaten cheese before. In the light of Giraldus' clear propaganda motives it might be wiser to take the more civilized Arabs' opinion. As they were in Spain for centuries, and as Ireland had always traded with that country, it is likely that they were actually more familiar with the island – certainly with the west coast – than were the neighbouring British, to whom it was a *terra* fairly *incognita*.

However, since those years, the possibility of Ireland rediscovering its maritime past, and also its Atlantean links, has been made difficult by a kind of scholarly wall that has surrounded the island for centuries. The process of isolating the Irish from their sea-girt existence probably began when Spain threatened England in the late sixteenth century. Ireland was a useful foothold on England's western flank. The first direct Spanish attempt on England was forestalled by the destruction of the Armada in 1588. Three years later, they tried the indirect way by landing at Kinsale in southern Ireland and forming an alliance with Irish chieftains. This also failed. The Spanish then appear to have given up their ambitions in this direction and reverted to peaceful trading with the island. They were replaced by the French who in the eighteenth century made two landings in force, one at Bantry in the south-west and the other at Killala in the north-west. These were also unsuccessful. England's increased sensitivity to attack from this quarter was expressed in the building of large granite watch-towers called martello towers. These are still to be seen on the coasts of Ireland.

As late as 1916, the continental rivals of England perceived Ireland as a stepping-stone to their ambitions. In that year, a submarine attempted to land arms on the coast of Kerry. The operation was a failure; the Irish representative on board the submarine, which had come all the way from Germany, was captured and hanged. These incidents tell less about the general aspirations of the Irish towards freedom than about the opportunism of the European powers. As one of Good Queen Bess's ministers once said to her: 'Whoever holds Ireland, holds a dagger to England's heart.'

It is no wonder that the Irish were discouraged from looking towards the sea. Over those centuries, the activities of Barbary pirates were also a threat to the status quo. It must have been obvious to the English and their Dublin agents that the native Irish must be kept from an awareness of the sea as a potential ally.

The maritime history of Ireland has been all but ignored in schools. Such a preoccupation appears to have been too materialistic for an education system based on a purely literary and religious perception of reality. When Irish schoolchildren are taught that pirates brought St Patrick from Britain to Ireland they are left in ignorance as to who these pirates were, how widespread was their activity, what other plunder they collected and what other places they sailed to. It is not usually emphasized that these mariners were Irish and constituted a serious threat to the Roman Empire.

'Prior to the age of the Vikings,' wrote an American scholar of this period, 'the Irish proved themselves to be the most intrepid mariners of the Atlantic.' He is not referring to the innocuous Irish monks, brave as they were in their frail currachs. As early as 222 AD, Irish sailors made their first recorded overseas excursion. It began a long period of raids across the Irish Sea to Roman-held Britain. Such were their depredations that the Romans found it necessary to build fortresses and watch-towers on the Isle of Anglesey as well as on both sides of the Bristol Channel, the most important one being situated at Cardiff. They thought it was wise to base a defensive flotilla at the mouth of the Severn as well as several fleets off the Cumberland coast.

Ireland was not always a kind of sponge, passively absorbing the various invaders; there was a two-way traffic and, in the period from the second to seventh centuries, appears to have been more outward than inward. How far afield they ranged is hard to establish but they certainly got as far as Bordeaux. Who knows but they might have anticipated the feats of the Vikings and gone as far as the Mediterranean. It would not have been in the interests of the historians of the period, or indeed of interest to them at all, to record such voyages.

For fear I might give the impression that the Irish were single-handedly disrupting the Roman Empire, I should give credit to other groups who were similarly plaguing Britain. The Picts of Scotland were a formidable naval force. They attacked both north-east and north-west Britain. Meanwhile, Anglo-Saxon pirates were in control of the east coast of Britain. Between these three groups – quite apart from the revolts of the indigenous peoples – the Romans in Britain had a hard time.

In 367 AD, their three main foes launched a major attack on the north of England. It may have been in connection with 'barbarian' raids like this, both in Britain and on the Continent, that the emperor decided things needed tightening up. Theodosius formulated a commercial code which detailed precisely where and when people could leave and enter the Empire, what goods they could bring in and out and exactly what taxes or duty should be paid on such goods. He eventually brought in passports. He thus hoped to control the barbarian world's trade and counteract the growing anarchy.

One of the last continental tribes the Romans conquered was the Veneti – the predecessors of those modern Atlanteans, the Bretons. The Veneti had their headquarters in that part of Armorica, or Brittany, where Gavr'inis – first cousin of New-grange – still stands. Nearby is the modern city of Brest, now headquarters of the French Navy.

Even though the Romans imitated the shallow boats of the Veneti, they could not quite conquer them because the tribe specialized in a form of guerrilla warfare on water. Their strongholds were built on peninsulae and took a lot of effort and manpower to capture. But, as soon as the Romans looked like gaining one peninsula, the Veneti simply boarded their ships and moved to the next, defying Caesar until he could build more sea-barriers, slowly transfer his forces and begin the whole process again. The Veneti were masters of the art of sailing; the Romans relied on banks of oars. The Veneti sails were made of tough hide which could withstand the force of Atlantic gales and their boats were shallow enough to capitalize on their intimate knowledge of every creek and rock on this 'côte sauvage'. The Romans eventually overcame the Veneti but the Veneti, then the Bretons, continued to be part of the Atlantean maritime world.

The Atlantean peoples were constantly in contact with one another, trading and exchanging ideas. An Irishman was responsible for the principal method of mussel cultivation in western France. In 1235, an Irish sailor named Walton was shipwrecked in the Bay of Aiguillon, near La Rochelle. He settled down to make a living by trapping birds in a net stretched across the mud flats of an estuary. In order to make the net secure he bedded it deeply in the mud and secured it with poles. However, being an observant man, he soon noticed that the poles became covered with mussel spawn. As he was as adaptable as observant, he soon switched to growing mussels. He was thus responsible for the proliferation of this form of fish farming. It is now a large industry on these Atlantic coasts of France and Spain.

When the Emperor Theodosius proclaimed limited entry and exit points for his Empire he must have inflated the value of the services of those seafarers on the fringes. When his civil servants in 374 AD thought it a good idea to prohibit the movement of bronze, gold and iron across the frontiers, many a smuggler must have giggled in his sea cabin. When, in 381 AD, the imperial bureaucrats pronounced that 'loyal friendly people' could export to the Empire on payment of a customs levy of fifteen per cent they forgot that such qualities as loyalty and friendship have very limited application in the world of commerce.

There developed in these areas what has been described by Archibald R. Lewis as 'an Atlantic Economic Community in the west, extending far beyond Rome's frontiers'.

Thus, while Caesar and his successors were having their triumphs, and promulgating laws whether they were obeyed or not, the Irish and Pictish and Anglo-Saxon maritime power grew. Within the economic community of the Atlantic reaches there were movements of people which left their mark. The Irish intrusions on Britain resulted in settlements in Wales and Cornwall; the displacement of the incumbents eventually resulted in the colonization of Armorica. In Northern Britain, colonists from Ireland formed a community called the Dal Riada and gave Pictland its modern name, Scotland. The Isle of Man was another Irish colony; the Manx language is still closer to Gaelic than to Welsh.

In summary, the Roman laws designed to injure economies outside the Empire had the reverse effect; they increased the incentives to sidestep those laws through smuggling. They must have given a big boost to the commerce of the Atlanteans. As we know from the much later period of the Barbary corsairs, this became the pattern of the Atlantic seaways: unorthodox and energetic. Strabo, a Latin writer of the second century, commented on the volume of traffic conducted by the native population – not the Romans – between Clausentum in the south of England and Cadiz in the south of Spain. From the southern areas came wine, salt and olive oil; from the north in return was sent iron, copper, lead, silver and hides. These items of exchange were also the basis of Galway's traditional prosperity.

A couple of years ago I visited La Coruna in Galicia. A feature of the town is an ancient lighthouse, considered to be the oldest surviving Roman construction of its kind. It is now called the Hercules Tower but in the fourth century it was known as the Portus Brittaniae, confirming the two-way traffic between Spain and the British Isles. Orosius in the fifth century also referred to the lighthouse and said it was sited 'ad speculam Brittaniae'. It can be assumed that when classical writers referred to Britain, the island of Ireland was included.

The considerable maritime activity up and down these coasts is also shown by the vast variety of ships and boats attributed to the various peoples. The Picts used two types: the coracle which was made of skin, and the 'ponto' which was more stoutly constructed. It was flat-bottomed, made of oak, had a high poop and stern and featured leather sails and an iron anchor. Even some of the skin-covered boats used by both Picts and Irish were not the frail craft we always imagine. According to another Latin writer, Sidonius, they were constructed of twenty to thirty hides, three hides thick. They had masts and could carry twenty passengers – possibly in addition to crew. About 550 AD the Irish started building stronger, wooden ships. These included the ocean-going 'barca'; a warship which is referred to as the navis longa; the caupullus; the navicula, which might be the antecedent of the present-day 'naomhōg' of Kerry; the navis onera; the scapha; finally, the domestic currach.

Caesar had already described the ships of the Veneti which he imitated, just as his predecessors had imitated the ships of the Carthaginians. The bows of the Veneti ships were unusually high to enable them to survive heavy seas and gales. Their hulls were made entirely of oak which rendered them immune to the ramming techniques of naval warfare. The cross timbers, he said, were made of beams a foot wide and fastened with iron as thick as a man's thumb. They even used iron chains to attach their anchors.

When the Romans finally extricated themselves from Britain around the year 407 AD, it is commonly assumed that chaos resulted. This is because the well-known classical world exited and formal written accounts of subsequent events became scarce. What this really means is that the normal, pre-existing – or even co-existing – cultural and trade contacts resumed their course without the paternal supervision of the Empire. Conventional history regards the ensuing period as the Dark Ages, the period when the 'barbarian' uprooted civilization. The Visigoths sacked Rome in 410 AD; they dominated north-west Spain in 419 AD; the Vandals swept down through Europe as far as Gibraltar, crossed the Straits and reached Carthage in 429; the Franks expanded over Gaul in 450; the Huns pushed all before them.

The only people who might be said to have been discommoded by this healthy rearrangement of property were subsequent historians: 'barbarians' do not leave written records to defend their actions. As a cynical Arab once remarked: 'The soldiers fight their battles; the peoples trade in peace; whoever likes can claim the world.'

The Atlantean probably only heaved a sigh of relief at the departure of the Romans. Certainly, it could not have made much difference to the Irish who had escaped the heavy hand of Empire, while, at the same time, reaping the unofficial fringe benefits. The trade that continued up and down the Atlantic coasts may have constituted the only cultural continuity in Europe – just as Ireland preserved a continuity of Western scholarship. 'Learning,' as a well-known historian once said, 'fled to the bogs of Ireland.'

There is one group of seafarers who have not yet been mentioned in the downfall of Roman Britain. This is because they were hovering off-stage, waiting for the inevitable moment when the erstwhile pirates would settle down and they themselves could take over the mantle of marauders. They were called the 'Heruls'; they originated in Scandinavia and they were the forerunners of the men who, from the seventh century onwards, would dominate the Atlantic seaways and make Ireland their base – the Vikings.

The records of Viking influence on Ireland were written by monks who portray the invaders as blood-thirsty destroyers. The Vikings were not Christian: they built the first secular towns in Ireland; Dublin itself was, at first, a Danish kingdom after centuries as a mere river crossing. Wicklow, Wexford, Waterford and many other places other owe their names to the Vikings.

The Vikings were in contact with cultures beyond the Atlanteans. In the seventh century, a new silver coinage began to appear in these Atlantic regions of the Friesian Islands, Britain and Ireland, Gaul and Spain. The largest hoard of such coins was found on the north-west coast of England, an area dominated by Viking kingdoms and trading intimately with Dublin. The Cuerdale Hoard is dated to the years 902–20 AD and contains an immense number of foreign coins of which thirty-one are Kufic Muslim dirhans. It is assumed that they were buried at the time of a quarrel between the Vikings here and their cousins in Ireland. Similar, smaller hoards have been found in Ireland in places as disparate as Derry, Lugga, Drogheda, Claremont and Kildare. These contained the Muslim dirhans also. Fourteen hundred Arab coins dating from Viking times have been found in the Aland Islands in the Baltic.

The significance of these coins is that, though they indicate links with the Middle East, most of them did not come by the Atlantic trade routes. But neither did they come overland. While the Norse and Danes were expanding westwards and establishing colonies in Scotland, Ireland, England, even in Gaul, their fellow-Scandinavians, the Swedes, were opening up trade routes in the opposite direction. They over-ran the eastern Baltic and penetrated south from Lake Ladoga on the rivers Volkhov and Lovat meeting the Dnieper which flows out into the Black Sea. Another route, via Lake Beloya, links to the Volga and hence the Caspian Sea; from the southern shore of the Caspian, a land route led to Baghdad; there the Vikings acquired the silver coins which, eventually, turned up as far west as Ireland. In 839, the Byzantine Emperor Theophilus met the western Emperor Louis the Pious at Ingelhiem taking with him a group of Vikings who had lost many men fighting Khazars on the inland waterways; they preferred to return by a safer route. In 921, Ibn Fadlan, ambassador from the Caliph Muktedir in Baghdad to the Bulgars, witnessed and recorded the gruesome ceremony of a Viking boat burial on the Volga. His description corresponds to the boat grave opened at Valsgärd in Denmark.

The key, as always, is travel by water, whether on the Atlantic seaways or on inland rivers. It suggests a picture of Europe which actually equates to early maps of the world in which the central area, the Mediterranean lands, are surrounded by a vast river which encircles and limits the known world of the time. This vast river was a much-travelled trade route – up the Atlantic coasts, across the Baltic, down the eastern rivers to the

Caspian and Black Seas and thence into the Mediterranean, to link up once more with the Atlantic. But this picture is at variance with the standard image of Europe which implies civilization at the centre and chaos at the fringes. It implies that, without the seaborne and highly structured activity on the perimeter, the centre of Europe would never have acquired its luxuries: spices, silks, wines etc which came from the Orient. This image helps me further to visualize the island of Ireland as less a remote speck in the Atlantic than, as the Vikings demonstrated, an important part of a circular trading network.

There is a famous coin in the British Museum which suggests that this trading went beyond simple commercial contact. This coin is a gold dinar – a Muslim coin – which has the name 'Offa' clearly stamped on it. Offa is the name of an eighth-century king of Mercia, England, the man to whom 'Offa's Dyke' – a 120-mile-long barrier between England and Wales – is credited. What is unusual about the coin is that it has an Arabic inscription: 'God is most Great; He has no companion'. This is a common Muslim expression. One explanation for this coin is that it is an imitation of the only gold currency with which King Offa was familiar – that used by the Muslims in Spain. It is agreed to be an imitation because there are mistakes in the Arabic which no Muslim would permit. Further, the name 'Offa' is imprinted upside down in relation to the Arabic.

The most prosaic reason for an Anglo-Saxon king striking such a coin is that he needed it to trade with a Moorish Spain at the height of its prosperity. What is odd about this explanation is that the rest of Europe is supposed to have been at complete loggerheads with the Muslims in Spain. When Offa's dinar is taken in conjunction with the Arabic-inscribed, ninth-century cross found in southern Ireland, it suggests that the residents in these islands were in continuing touch with Muslim Spain. The image of a homogeneous Christian Europe having nothing to do with an equally homogeneous, but Muslim, world is a gross over-simplification.

The internal tensions of Europe throughout the Middle Ages, and the way they impinged on Ireland, must have been greatly overshadowed by what was perceived as a common threat: the Muslim presence. Islam dominated the area from Samarkand, through the entire Middle East, across the Mediterranean southern shores and up to the borders of Spain and France.

In so far as Ireland and the Iberian peninsula were in direct maritime contact – however sporadic – from Neolithic times onwards, it must be conceded that the eight-hundred-year Muslim presence in the peninsula had to have some effect on the northern island. For a few sparkling centuries in the Middle Ages, Ireland was the Light of the West, the acknowledged preserver of all that was of value to Western civilization. It is no coincidence that this was also one of the periods of brilliance in the Muslim courts of Cordoba, Toledo and Granada.

# chapter nine

The Visigoth kingdoms of Spain fell to the Moors in 711–12 AD; the invasion was launched by the governor of North Africa, Nursa Ibn Nusovir, and led by a Berber, Tariq Ibn Zayyad. Berbers were granted control of the colder northern areas of Spain on the borders of Asturias and Galicia, while the Arabs sensibly kept the sunnier south for themselves. Moorish Spain became the most advanced and civilized place in Europe: the Arabs brought with them from the East, the philosophy and science of Greece, the literary and political wisdom of Persia and the medicine and mathematics of India. Between the seventh and tenth centuries in Spain there was a period of relative peace in which learning flourished. Such a period again occurred in the twelfth and fourteenth centuries. Over this entire era a culture developed which was unequalled in Europe. Indeed, without this Muslim foundation, the age of Scholasticism and the European Renaissance are unlikely to have happened at all. Besides Muslim Spain, there was only one other place in Europe which had not sunk into 'barbarism' and in which learning was at a premium. This was the island of Ireland which, between the seventh and tenth centuries, also enjoyed a Golden Age. This was the period when Irish art achieved its pinnacle – when it earned the accolade 'Island of Saints and Scholars'.

The inherent genius of the people of the island expressed itself in illustrated manuscripts, stone-carving, metalwork and pure scholarship. According to many scholars, anything that was worth learning – Latin, Greek, arithmetic, geometry, astronomy, natural sciences, logic – all could be studied in the monasteries of Lismore, Bangor, Clonfert, Clonard and Armagh. European scholars flocked to the island to learn. The Venerable Bede records that English scholars of the period came to study under Irishmen. Since the sixth century, Irish scholars had also been travelling to Europe, to bring some kind of rekindling of the spark of a shattered learning and civilization. A Gallic scholar of the year 873 AD referred to 'the whole of Ireland with its flock of philosophers, contemning the danger of the sea, coming to Gaul'. These philosophers were also described as manifesting 'a sense of superiority which was held to be irritatingly characteristic of the Irish' and 'a certain exotic use of language also associated with Irish learning'. Irish scholars travelled as far as Tarentum in the south and Kiev in the east: the Norse depredations increased the flow of travelling scholars taking manuscripts to safety.

People have agonized for years about how such a 'remote' island could have achieved such a degree of sophistication. Traditionally-minded Irish scholars have put it down to native genius inherited from the ubiquitous 'Celts'. The British have implied that, actually, the real development was in Northumbria whose achievements in art and scholarship were carried to Ireland but Bede undermines that assumption. Continentals say it was Gallic scholars on the run from the barbarians, who were responsible; they escaped to Ireland, bringing their talents with them. The Irish, becoming protective, tended to refuse any credit to outside influences.

In this century, scholars have increasingly acknowledged the presence of oriental influences in the Ireland of the period. This is usually explained by reference to Christian Byzantium and the possibility of that art being doled out to western Europe through the medium of Rome. But as Michael Ryan – author of a paper on the latest treasure found in Ireland, the Derrynaflan Chalice – says, there is a significant difference between these Irish chalices and their west European equivalents of the same period. The entire Latin West interposed itself between Ireland and the Greek Byzantine Empire, so how could this oriental influence have been mediated so directly to an island in the Atlantic if not via the Mediterranean? From the seventh century on, the Muslims controlled the Straits of Gibraltar.

Prominent among the great scholars of this period is the philosopher John Scottus Eriugena who left his native Ireland before 847 to settle in the Frankish kingdom of Charles the Bald. He was described as the greatest metaphysician of all time and part of his uniqueness lay in his familiarity with Greek and oriental matters, a familiarity which was unusual in western Europe. Usually this talent of his was explained by saying he must have lived in the East for a long time and received his literary and philosophical training there. One author decided he must even be a Greek because of his knowledge of that school of philosophy. His mastery of Greek, Chaldean and Arabic was also attributed to a long stay in Athens. Not in any part of the discussion I read on this man was there a reference to Muslim Spain.

Now that seemed peculiar to me because I learned that the Arabs claimed almost a monopoly of Greek learning which was acquired in their conquest of the Middle East and, particularly in this context, Alexandria – long the seat of Greek scholarship. Pagan Greek philosophy was not popular with the established Christian Church because its emphasis on ethics and reason tended to undermine a system of authority based on faith. A famous school of philosophy in Athens was even closed in the sixth century for this reason. Probably the last translation into Latin of the works of Aristotle and Plato was not available until Thomas Aquinas commissioned it in the thirteenth century. In the meantime, the Arabs had the Greek writings translated by Syrian scholars and they became the foundation of their immense strides in all the sciences; the Arab world was united by language and religion, ideas could travel quickly from Baghdad to Cordoba. Further, because Moorish Spain was quite a distance from the formal centres of Islamic orthodoxy, it soon developed an autonomy which enabled it to encourage independent scholarly investigation. At precisely the same time as Eriugena was impressing the Frankish court with his grasp of Eastern languages, philosophy and cosmology (and incidentally making them nervous with his denial of the existence of Hell), Muslim scholars were paralleling his findings in Spain.

Hunayn Bin Ishaq, a medical doctor, was the greatest ever scholar in the history of Islamic translation. Prior to approaching a Greek work he would collate various manuscripts in order to establish a sound basic text. He placed the art of translation on a healthy scientific footing. This man and his team translated the complete medical works of Hippocrates and Galen, almost all of Aristotle, and he was responsible for most of Plato being translated. His thorough approach to Greek learning paved the way for a series of brilliant Muslim scholars: Ya'qub Al Kindi (d. 866) who, like Eriugena, tried to harmonize the findings of philosophy with the teachings of dogma. He subscribed to the idea that 'true religion is true philosophy'. Another, Abu Bakr Ar-Razi, delved into cosmology and the transmigration of souls – a thesis which Eriugena also favoured and which in Gallic circles was considered daring. A succession of Muslim scholars of Spain culminated in Ibn Khaldoun, a fourteenth-century social-philosopher – the 'Father of Sociology'.

It is ironic that, in the thirteenth century, intellectual Europe was dominated by a philosophic controversy between the followers of Averroes and Avicenna – both of whom were Muslim philosophers. These two names are an illustration of what I came to interpret as a lack of European acknowledgement of its indebtedness to Islamic learning. The names Ibn Rushd, Ibn Sina, Ibn Bajja are unfamiliar in Europe. This is because they have been presented to us in Latin form: Averroes, Avicenna, Avempace etc. It may be an innocent way of homogenizing the world of scholarship but it has led to ignorance of Europe's debt to Arab scholars.

Eriugena was a prolific man whose ideas were largely influenced by, and incorporated, Neo-Platonism. Later, this would be a distinguishing feature between East and West in that Europe would plump for the cold logic of Aristotle while the East would retain the mystic possibilities of Neo-Platonism. The latter took a much kindlier view of man, his potential for good and his ultimate destination. Eriugena followed the belief that people who live according to right reason, be they atheists or not, are capable of salvation. By his reckoning, even a pagan like Socrates could be saved. This suggestion had serious implications for the doctrine of original sin, never mind the implicit suggestion that the graces supplied by an established Church might be superfluous. If a man could be saved by his own efforts it made priests redundant. It was reminiscent of the experience of another reputed Irishman, Pelagius, who centuries before had raised the same questions. He was tried for heresy and, incidentally, defended himself in fluent Syriac. History repeated itself in 855 when at the synod of Valence, Eriugena's *On the Divisions of Nature* was condemned. The more I discovered about these early Irish scholars, the greater grew the impression of men working on the fringe of orthodoxy, of trying to bridge the gap between faith and reason which, despite their efforts, ended up as an abyss.

Similar tensions applied to Muslim philosophers of the period. In Spain, because of its physical distance from the centres of Islamic orthodoxy in the East, there was an open-mindedness in their thinking. Occasionally, the strict tenets of Islamic dogma did impinge on their researches, when they had to work hard at showing there was no essential conflict between dogma and philosophy. One man, Al-Ghazzali, was able to distinguish between aspects of Greek/Arab philosophy which he thought were not inimical to religion; these were logic and mathematics. Physics and metaphysics, on the other hand, were in a dangerously grey area. I found it striking that, in so far as I understood these complex concepts, Irish Christians and the Muslims of Spain were using the same intellectual tools to extend their deeply religious, sometimes mystic ideas beyond the narrow confines of their respective orthodoxies. I found it ironic to read the following in a book about the Berbers in Arabic literature: 'The Berber dissenter and the Berber "holy man" or marabout often appears in Arabic literature in a guise and with a temperament not dissimilar to the Celtic saint in Ireland, Wales or Brittany in the Dark Ages . . . '

Arab historians say that European scholars flocked to the centres of learning like Cordoba, Toledo and Seville. In the early eighth century, Charlemagne had discreetly retreated from a major attack on Muslim Spain. The decision was made partly because he learned that the various Arab factions were united for once, partly because word came of a Saxon revolt on his eastern frontier. He may also have heard that the Arabized Christians of Spain, the 'Mozarabes', were also prepared to resist him. It indicates that these Mozarabes preferred living in Muslim Spain to the possible domination of a northern Christian emperor. However, the point is that from then on, for many years, there was a stand-off between the Christian North and the Muslim South, with little formal contact between the two cultures. How, then, was European scholarship so influenced by developments in Spain?

From the sixth century onwards it had been the itinerant Irish scholars who had revived the weakly learning and even Christianity itself in Europe. They founded monasteries and schools of learning in England, France, Belgium, Germany, Switzerland, Austria and Italy. Their unorthodox form of Christianity was also quite novel in Europe. The so-called 'Celtic' Church celebrated Easter on the same date as the Alexandrians, a date which was at variance with Rome. They preserved their own form of tonsure or hairstyle. They were criticized by a pope who was distressed to find these shabby itinerants become so popular with the people. They seemed also to have an independent frame of mind: one of them, Fearghall, became Bishop of Salzburg in 784 and proceeded to announce that there were people with souls at the opposite side of the world. As this had implications for their salvation – had they even heard of Christ? – Fearghall was accused of heresy by the Anglo-Saxon papal legate, Boniface. However, in the ensuing trial, Fearghall won.

From whence did Ireland derive this form of Christianity which showed an independence of mind so much at variance with the orthodox western Church? It lasted until the twelfth century when the Anglo-Normans, with a papal authorization, crossed from Britain. If my general thesis is anywhere near the truth, then Ireland was in constant contact with the ideas and cultures of the Mediterranean, both northern and southern shores. This, as I have tried at length to show, was because of the convenience of the Atlantic seaways. From the seventh, right up to the seventeenth century, events in Spain were so profound that they must have had some, even indirect, effect on the island.

The Islamic achievement on the peninsula was impressive. With unparalleled wealth at their disposal – the partial fruits of an empire that stretched 3000 miles – it looked as if nothing could stop the Arabs. Indeed, there was one precise moment in history when it was quite in the balance whether, as one author put it, 'Europe would be Christian or Muslim, whether the future Notre Dame or the future St Paul's would ring to the chant of the muezzin'.

This author, Stanley Lane Poole, was quite serious. He described one battle as one of the fifteen most important ever fought in history. This was in 733 when Charles Martel stopped the advance of the Arabs between Poitiers and Tours in France. They had already seized Bordeaux and Narbonne and, in fact, would hold the latter for another sixty years. With their tough Berber warriors, their superb horsemen and an uncluttered faith, very little could oppose them. As late as 890 they were settling in Provence and making raids on eastern Switzerland. A feature of one of the Swiss cantons is still called 'La Bisse des Sarrasins'. Their presence in France is still remembered in the word 'troubadour' which derives from 'tarab dour', an Arabic phrase meaning House of Delight. From this seminal Troubadour musical form grew a tradition which, oddly, has a

vestigial expression in both Brittany and Conamara. This consists of an improvised duet between two singers, usually humorous. In Brittany,
it is called Kan ha Diskan; in Conamara, they
know it as Lūibīnī. The European tradition of
romantic chivalry, with its heroic knights and
sighing princesses, derives directly from the
Arabs, who adapted the desert bedouin's horsemanship and code of honour.

After Charles Martel's success, the Arabs and
their Berber forces retrenched in Spain and concentrated on developing the garden of Spain into a
sort of heaven on earth; indeed, their idea of
paradise is still a garden, with plenty of sparkling
fountains and streams. They have not often been
as near to paradise as they were in Andalusia.
They built palaces, mosques, libraries, hospitals,
entire towns. By the tenth century Cordoba is
reputed to have had a population of 150,000 which
was served by 700 mosques and 900 public baths.
Cleanliness, for the Muslim, was next to godliness.
In Christianity, on the other hand, the odour of
sanctity attributed to saints was usually due to
their not washing. After the fall of Moorish Spain,
Phillip II – husband of the English Queen Mary
– ordered the destruction of all Muslim baths
because they were a symbol of the infidels. The
Arab engineers developed irrigation systems
which enabled fruits and flowers to grow where
nothing grew before – and, in some cases, where
nothing has grown since.

Cordoba was the crowning glory of Muslim
Spain and its mosque became the jewel in that
crown. This architectural wonder was begun in
784 AD by Abd Er Rahmen, the Ummayad Caliph,
who spent 80,000 pieces of gold on it – the
proceeds of battle with the Goths. His son completed the work in 793 with the proceeds of the
sack of Narbonne. The building was described by

Stanley Lane Poole in 1900:

Each succeeding Sultan added some new beauty to the building, which is one of the finest examples of early Saracenic art in the world. One put gold on the columns and walls; another added a new minaret; another built a fresh arcade to hold the swelling congregations.

Nineteen is the number of the arcades from east to west, and thirty-one from north to south; twenty-one doors encrusted with shining brass admitted the worshippers; 1293 columns support the roof, and the sanctuary was paved with silver and inlaid with rich mosaics, and its clustered columns were carved and inlaid with gold and lapis lazuli.

The pulpit was constructed of ivory and choice woods, in 36,000 separate panels, many of which were encrusted with precious stones and fastened with gold nails. Four fountains for washing before prayer, supplied with water from the mountains, ran night and day. Hundreds of brass lanterns made out of Christian bells illumined the mosque at night. [These bells were taken from Santiago de Campostella and carried south on the shoulders of prisoners. When the Muslims were defeated the bells were returned, this time on the shoulders of Muslim prisoners.]

Three hundred attendants burnt sweet-smelling ambergris and aloes wood in the censers, and prepared the scented oil which fed the ten thousand wicks of the lanterns. Much of the beauty of this mosque still remains.

Travellers stand amazed among the forest of columns which open out in apparently endless vistas on all sides. The porphyry, jasper and marbles are still in place; the splendid glass mosaics, which artists from Byzantium came to make, still sparkle like jewels on the walls.

As one stands before the loveliness of the Great Mosque, the thought goes back to the days of the glories of Cordova, the palmy days of the Great Khalif, which will never return.

Many centuries later a Christian church was crudely placed in the centre of the mosque. It was described by Titus Burckhardt as 'like a giant black spider' which, he said, was 'in marked contrast to the clear and innate harmony that emanates from the form of the Islamic structure'.

The influence of Byzantine artists on Muslim art and architecture resulted from diplomatic exchanges in 839 AD. It shows that at least half of Christendom – the eastern half – was able to communicate with Islam. If one bears in mind the propensity of Irish Christians for eastern attitudes – as exemplified by Eriugena – and the fact that their greatest artistic achievements have Byzantine echoes, the position of Muslim Spain becomes more significant for the island. There had been a schism between Rome and Byzantium in the sixth century. It was never completely healed and was formalized in 1084. The iconoclastic row, during which artists were forbidden to make human representations, must have driven many of them out of Byzantium.

An attack on Seville – only five years after Cordoba's diplomatic exchange with Byzantium – by the Vikings shows that the Atlantic seaways were functioning very well. It is also recorded that soon after this attack the Caliphate of Cordoba sent a diplomatic mission to the Norsemen, in Zealand. There can be no doubt that contact, whether aggressive or friendly, was still maintained between this island and Spain.

There were examples of the clear co-operation that existed between members of different religions during the Moorish reign. The Jews were among the scholars employed by the Muslims and they enjoyed, according to Burckhardt, their finest intellectual flowering since their dispersal from Palestine to foreign lands. The two Semitic peoples, Jews and Arabs, when they co-operated in Spain – under an Islamic authority – were a powerful scholarly combination. The most prominent Jewish scholar was Moshe Ben Maimon, or Moses Maimonides, who was born in Cordoba in 1135 AD and produced works like the *Guide to the Perplexed*. This occupies as important a place in Judaism as the works of Thomas Aquinas in Catholicism. Maimonides followed the example of Eriugena and many others in incorporating the philosophy of the Greeks in his work.

The Mozarabes – the Arabized Christians of Spain – were so integrated with the Islamic state that when Abd Er Rahmen wanted an emissary to visit the court of Otto I as well as Constantinople and Syria, he chose a Mozarabe Bishop, Rabi Ben Zaid, known to Europeans as Recemundus. Christians had, for centuries, been torn apart on the doctrine of the Trinity. It was the root cause of many 'heresies' and excommunications. With its insistence on the divinity of Jesus Christ, it was infinitely more inimical to Muslims and Jews whose basic tenet was one incomparable God. In an effort to ease theological tensions between Arab, Jew and Christian, the Archbishop Elipandus of Seville in 784 proclaimed a doctrine of 'adoption' for Jesus. In doing this he showed his beliefs were much closer to eastern Christianity than to that of the West. Predictably, his idea was condemned in Rome and at synods throughout northern Europe. An Asturian monk named

Beatus composed a commentary on the subject illustrated with what are termed remarkable pictures and copied many times by Andalusian monks who had emigrated to the Christian north of Spain.

According to Burckhardt, these pictures 'are a curious blend of early Christian, Mediterranean and Asiatic elements, proving that despite their affiliation with Rome the Mozarabic communities were in closer contact with Christian communities in Palestine, Syria and Mesopotamia than with western Europe'.

In investigating Muslim Spain and the Mozarabic Christians, I constantly felt the temptation to attribute all that was wonderful in the brilliant period of Irish art to direct contact with this overlooked episode of European history. However, although from the point of view of chronology, I could safely speculate on Eriugena's sources there and also look for later influences on Irish art, there was a problem. The Arabs did not bring the aesthetic and intellectual treasures of the East to Spain until 711 AD. By then, the earliest formative influences on Irish art were already working on the island. So, although contact with Muslim Spain was likely to have had certain repercussions on the Irish, it could not explain everything about the Golden Age of Irish art.

# chapter ten

When Niall Fallon was researching his fine book on the Spanish Armada in Ireland, he was often struck by the accuracy with which local people could pinpoint the site of a particular wreck; in not one instance was the local tradition as to the precise position of a 400-year-old ship proved wrong. He suggested that 'too often historians have downgraded the accuracy with which these wrecks are remembered; it is a curious aberration of judgement which ignores the fact that native folklores and memory have a long recollection of local events, and while it may distort, it cannot alter the kernel of truth which is the centre of such legend'.

The monks who recorded the words of the Irish epics – and, as we know, re-arranged them – in the first instance, got them from story-tellers who had memorized them from others. The presence in a story-teller's house of people who are familiar with a tale might be an encouragement artistically to embellish the narration but they would be a deterrent to gross distortion. As David Greene has said: 'We must beware of seeing the old stories primarily as a form of entertainment . . . if stories were told, it was because they were believed to be true, and not from any conscious desire for literary expression.' So, I felt it to be a good idea to be at least aware of the stories, beliefs and mythologies that support the idea of a connection between Ireland and North Africa.

A Welsh chronicle relates that Britain was first colonized by Hu the Mighty 'who came over the sea from the Summer country'; in Brittany, the long lines of menhirs became the remains of an army of southern invaders; in Ireland, a particularly long upper lip was proof positive of a Milesian background; in North Africa, the existence of red-haired, blue-eyed people was attributed to the Irish. Even Stonehenge was reputed to have been built by Merlin the Magician who used stones from Naas in Ireland which originally came from Africa! In the Friesian islands, also part of the Atlantean area, there is a Santa Claus who is believed to come from Spain and travels with a servant called Black Pete who is a Moor. The Friesians also had the custom of dressing boys in skirts to ward off the fairies – who would not be interested in girls; this tradition was exactly duplicated in the Aran islands.

The original owners of the Cornish tin mines are traditionally supposed to have been of Semitic origin and direct descendants from the Phoenicians: they were banished in a pogrom by Edward the Confessor in the eleventh century. In 1833, a man named Joachim de Villaneuve wrote a book called *Phoenician Ireland* and maintained that Irish druids were the snake priests of those seafarers. Their god, Baal, can be connected with the Irish 'Balor of the Evil Eye' as well as to 'Beltine', Gaelic for the month of May which means the 'fire of Baal'.

An Irish clergyman, the Rev Robert Walsh who spent some time in Constantinople and who travelled widely in the Mediterranean in the nineteenth century, made some notes on a visit to Carteia in Spain:

[Tartessus] was probably the first city ever erected by a civilized people outside the Mediterranean, when the Phoenician Hercules rent asunder the mountains and opened for his enterprising companions a passage into the Atlantic.

My companion was very fond of Irish lore and had no doubt of the Phoenician origin of the Irish people. He therefore was assiduous in pointing out to me many circumstances about this town as confirming his opinion. We met several of the peasantry; the men rode always two on a horse or mule with the face of one close to the back of the other; the women sat on the offside, with the left leg to the neck of the beast. The head-dress of the females consisted of a scarf, or shawl, drawn over their caps and tied behind in a knot, the corners of which fell between their shoulders – all which peculiarities are still to be seen among the peasantry about the Milesian or Phoenician town of Galway at this day.

They have also many opinions in common which have their origin antecedent even to the time of the Romans. They imagine for instance that a sick man's life depends on the state of the tide, and that he never dies until it begins to ebb. This notion, which is mentioned by Aristotle and referred to by Pliny, is common in the West of Ireland and entertained even by many physicians there. These usages and opinions, he asserted, were proofs of the identity of the two peoples, not to say anything of the nondescript animal at the cistern, whose tail twines round its legs exactly like that of the extraordinary beast to be seen in the front of Cormac's very ancient chapel on the rock of Cashel. I have no doubt if our worthy friend, General Vallancey was still alive, he would make out a very respectable theory from these data.

The Rev Robert Walsh had a healthy scepticism about these suggested links but at least his account indicates that these impressions existed in Spain, too. Actually, the rich designs on the Galway shawl are derived from Spain. He did not mention the cloak worn traditionally by women of West Cork. It was called 'an Fallaing Mhuimhneach' which means Munster cloak and has frequently been likened to the Arab burnous.

Such speculation is not confined to the nineteenth century. In 1937, J. Foster Forbes presented a series of lectures on the BBC entitled *The Unchronicled Past.* The subject was the archaeology of the British Isles and referred to the Iberians who 'sailed up from Spain and Portugal and moved in [to Britain] from the Atlantic. But they can be traced much further afield than Spain and Portugal; they came, it is now confidently believed, from Egypt.'

He then quotes Sir Norman Lockyer who 'was led by his astronomical enquiries to conclude that the people who reached Britain four thousand years ago had evidently communicated to them a very complete Egyptian culture'.

So, [J. Foster Forbes continued], you must imagine these ancient Egyptians sailing down the Mediterranean or pausing for a while on the Northern shores of Africa, and so on, out through the Straits of Gibraltar, in their search for precious stones and metals. It must surely have been these people to whom mythology refers as the Ancient Mariners who passed through the Pillars of Hercules in search of the Garden of the Hesperides.

The tradition of an Egyptian connection with the British Isles frequently recurs in folk tales. Between Ireland and that area there seems to have been much coming and going. In the *Book of Invasions of Ireland* – the *Lebor Gabāla Ērenn* – there are details of the voyage of the early 'Irish' from

Egypt and Libya to Crete and Sicily, thence to Spain and onwards to Ireland. Perhaps J. Foster Forbes was relying on this concoction of legend. Still, according to Arbois de Juvainville – author of *Cours de Literature Celtigue* – the Irish were called 'Egyptian' both by themselves and others during the Middle Ages. This may have been simply a way of distinguishing their brand of Christianity from that of Western Europe. The prehistoric invaders the Fir Bolg were said to have spent two centuries in exile in the east after being driven out of Ireland by the Fomorians: the Fir Bolg returned to overwhelm the Fomorians and then they were again driven out by another invader, again from the east, the Milesians.

Kenny's Bookshop in Galway presented me with a dusty treatise: *Irish Wizards in the Woods of Ethiopia*. It was written by an American and had the alternative title 'An Enquiry into the Meaning of God'. It took the view that many references in Irish sagas had their equivalent in Ethiopian folklore. It even invoked an ancient Irish hymn which referred to Brigid – an Irish pagan goddess who latterly turned into a saint – as the Queen of Sheba. The author, Winthrop Palmer Boswell, even saw a St Brigid's cross – fashioned in rushes – in Lalibela, an Ethiopian monastic centre. She pointed out that 'Banba', an old name for Ireland, is also the Ethiopian name for the baobab tree which is held in great reverence by both Ethiopians and Berbers. As a result, Boswell developed an interesting analogy between the tree culture of that part of Africa and the Druidic interest in yew and ash. She pointed out that the old Irish alphabet was based on the names of trees. However, as this particular argument was largely based on comparisons between words I was wary of it. When language changes, the first features to succumb are nouns – the syntax, as Heinrich

Wagner illustrated, can linger on indefinitely. An argument based almost entirely on similarities between nouns and adjectives in different languages – such as the above – gives the feeling of walking on shifting sands.

When etymologists get to work on word roots and endings it is almost impossible for a non-specialist to follow them through the thickets. All one can do is make an act of faith in their integrity and hope that the equivalent of market forces – their peer group – will keep a check on flights of the imagination. By contrast, there is nothing esoteric about folk tales or folklore, which, by definition, are accessible to everybody.

I came across one thorough student of this subject, E.L. Ranelagh, who went to immense trouble to show the close relationship between Eastern and Western versions of folk tales. One particular example was of great interest to me; it depended less on the truth or myth of the stories than on their essential similarity. These were accounts of the exploits and background of the two greatest heroes of Arabia and Ireland: Antar and Cū Chulainn.

They both spring from their respective 'heroic ages' although Antar is customarily given a historic reality as having existed in 600 AD. Cū Chulainn is simply ascribed to pre-Christian, pagan Ireland. They both are located in a cattle economy where the main activity appears to be rustling. The *Tāin Bō Cuailgne*, in which Cū Chulainn is immortalized, translates as the *Cattle Raid of Cooley*. Antar and Cū Chulainn both distinguish themselves as small boys by killing ferocious dogs. The Irish hero, whose original name was Séadanda, actually derived his title 'Hound of Culann' from the exploit. Both men were reared by single women – Antar by Zebeedah and Cū Chulainn by Scāthach. Both have arms conferred on them by close male relatives. Each of them can terrify the enemy with his eyes alone; Antar's grow monstrously red and protuberant with rage; Cū Chulainn draws one eye into his head and causes the other to stick out like a cauldron. It is in their deaths that they particularly are distinguished. Antar, badly wounded, deceives the enemy by sitting motionless on his trusty steed, Abjer, keeping himself upright by leaning on his spear. He thus guards the pass and allows his companions to escape. Cū Chulainn, also at the point of death in the Gap of Ulster, ties himself to a post and remains upright even though mortally wounded. It is only when a raven lights on his shoulder that his enemies know he no longer threatens them. Even their horses behave similarly: they charge the enemy to discourage an approach to their masters.

Generally speaking, these are archetypes of all heroes; it is in the detail that significant similarity lies. As a footnote to E.L. Ranelagh's researches, I discovered that another Irish story – that of Nuada of the Golden Arm – had its exact equivalent in an Arabian epic. The latter featured a famous pre-Islamic rain god called Hobbal who, like Nuada, lost an arm. It, too, was replaced with one made of gold. E.L. Ranelagh regarded the affinity between Irish and Arabian epics as remarkable because the early stories did not appear to have been mediated through normal Greek–Roman–Latin channels, ie through continental Europe. Further – and this particularly pleased me – not only was the Irish corpus of stories agreed to be the ultimate source of British epics such as the Arthurian legend but the early literature of Ireland, Britain and Iceland were considered to be independent of European heroic literature.

The European adoption of Muslim modes of chivalry and romance, in which are embedded so-called 'heroic' elements, did not occur until the

Middle Ages. Long before that there existed in Ireland the epic of Cū Chulainn and in Arabia the epic of Antar. If these stories were not mediated through Europe, by what route were they exchanged? This and similar matters continually puzzle scholars who assume that everything in Ireland and Britain had to come direct from the continent of Europe.

These stories existed before Christian monks began to write them down in the seventh century. What is in dispute is whether the oriental and classical references were brought in by the monks or were already present. Robin Flower stated one side of the case well:

These men of the new learning set themselves from an early date to consider how the Irish history which they had received from their predecessors, vivid in detail, but regrettably loose in chronology, might be fitted into the scheme of universal history which ruled the Latin Church. This scheme had been laid down once and for all by Christians in the chronicles of Eusebius . . . The theory at the base of this remarkable compilation was that the great world kingdoms – Assyria, Egypt, Palestine, Greece – had all by a divine providence led up to the Roman Empire which in its turn by the peace of the Church under Constantine had become the empire of Christ and had given the world constitution its final form. The actual arrangement of the chronicle corresponded to this conception. The whole history of the ancient world was set out in a series of parallel columns, one for each kingdom, and the events of each kingdom were synchronised so that the advance of history, century by century, could be followed at a glance for each kingdom and for all kingdoms.

It was a simple matter to add another column for Ireland, but much less simple to settle the chronology so that the Irish kings might appear in the succession and in a right relation to their contemporaries in the great world kingdoms.

These early historians and chroniclers were consequently known as 'synchronizers' or 'Fer Comgne' and it is clear that their version of history included references to the Middle East.

A body of historical material and stories must have existed before the monks appeared, to which the major European heroic epics were, at least, partly indebted; in which there were classical, oriental, even Indian echoes more likely to be accounted for by direct contact with North Africa, Spain and the Middle East than by any European, 'civilizing' intervention.

In re-reading these stories, there was another aspect which was very satisfying from my point of view: a large proportion of them was acted out in a maritime context. Indeed, one of the most prominent of the gods in these stories was Mananann Mac Lir, the equivalent of Neptune.

Their ocean-God was Mananann Mac Lir
Whose angry lips
in their snowy foam would oft inter
great fleets of ships.

It is appropriate that this god should be recalled in the name of the Isle of Man, Oileán Manann, which is located in the middle of the Irish Sea, obviously so that he could keep an eye on his Welsh, Irish and Scots subjects. Mananann is first encountered by an Irish voyager named Bran who is, typically, searching for an Isle of Joy. Suddenly he sees a strange figure riding the crest of a wave in a chariot. The stranger sings:

Bran thinks this is a marvellous sea.
For me it is a flowery plain.
Speckled salmon leap from the belly of your
    sea;
To me they are calves and sprightly lambs.

Mananann carried a bag made from the skin of a crane which purportedly contained the alphabet – an echo of the Phoenicians. The crane was, in fact, his wife Aoife who had earned his wrath by trying to steal the god's secret knowledge and tell it to the world. This story of the seventh century is healthily pagan. There are no pious monks braving all for the love of God; a simple hedonistic way of life is celebrated. But, by the ninth century, it has been expanded to become the voyage of Mael Dūin in which the hero has become pious enough to praise the Lord for his various deliverances. It still retains some lechery, as when Mael Dūin's companions try in vain to persuade a woman to sleep with their leader. However, towards the end they find a church and a grey-haired incumbent, a priest to whom Mael Dūin defers. Christianity has arrived! Predictably, not long after Mael Dūin, the same story becomes the vehicle solely for an account of a saint's wanderings. This is the *Voyage of St Brendan* which has been elsewhere detailed but which is the culmination of all Irish maritime escapades of the period.

References in many other stories show that the Irish, Welsh and Scots were not only familiar with the vagaries of the sea but that it was a normal part of their consciousness.

The sea is full, the wave is in flood, lovely is the home of ships; the sandbearing wind makes whirlpools round the island; fleet is the helm upon the broad sea.

The coastal folklore of Ireland is rich with bizarre encounters between seals and humans, sea-horses, huge eels, magic islands, mermaids, even sub-marine butter-making. Most of these stories are highlighted by pithy verses and sayings, some of which are happily risqué.

The three swiftest things in the sea are the seal, the mackerel and the ray; the three that leave the least trace are the bird on a branch, the ship on the sea and a man on a woman.

In one story a man named Connla will fall in love with a fairy woman and sail away in her crystal boat; in another the hero will mount a fine steed behind his lady love and they will both fly away over the sea. In one fantasy, a sailor named Ruadh is on his way with three ships and ninety men to meet the Norsemen near Scotland – the details are always necessary to give verisimilitude – when his ship is becalmed. He immediately knows what to do: he goes over the side and swims deep down until he meets nine women. With each of them he has to sleep before they will lift the spell that has immobilized his craft.

The frequent surrealism of these stories reaches its peak in an account of what happened to some monks in Clonmacnoise. They were praying in their chapel when they looked up and saw a ship sailing overhead, its anchor trailing. The anchor caught in a door and one of the crew descended, going through the motions of swimming. He released the anchor and was about to swim up when a priest caught him by the ankle, causing him to screech out: 'Let go, for God's sake, or I'll drown.' Released, he calmly swam up through the air, taking the anchor with him. The ship sailed smoothly away.

Even when they were beach-combing there had

to be an imaginative touch: when a woman was washed up on the shore in Ireland she was a giantess, fifty feet tall but with breasts unformed; in Scotland, in the same story, the woman becomes ninety-two feet in length. There are seventeen feet between her breasts and her nose is seven feet long. But 'every limb of her is as white as the down of a swan or the foam of the sea'.

Even centuries after the dutiful hand of ecclesiastical scribes had converted most of these stories into parables to lead the faithful to God, the power of the original could seep through. The richness and variety of Irish folk tales is one testimony of the tradition of the 'filī' or poets who disdained writing for fear their memory might atrophy. The noting down by clerics of these stories did not suddenly make these story-tellers redundant.

One of my first encounters in Conamara was with a well-known 'seanachaī', the late Beartlai O Conghaile. He was sitting in a tiny shop in the middle of the day, a child on each knee, reciting a story in Gaelic. It had the exaggeration, the repetition of phrases, the flowing phrases of the true story-teller. The tradition was still alive, a thousand years after the monks encountered it. An account of another story-teller in Kerry is full of pathos. This man had finally run out of an audience; they had been seduced away by cars, radios and television. But the craft was important enough for him to try and preserve it. So he could be seen driving the cows home on a summer's evening, reciting his stories to the midges and the unheeding backs of the cows. Fortunately, his stories and those of the other Irish 'seanachaī' have been largely preserved on tape and in notebooks so that a future, more appreciative, generation might enjoy them.

Possibly the most important myth in the context

of Atlanteans is that of Atlantis, the drowned continent. I tend to agree with Robert Graves that it is a pity that the term 'myth' has come to mean 'fanciful, absurd, unhistorical'. The poet maintained that myths are all 'grave records of ancient religious customs or events, and reliable enough as history once their language is understood'. Once their language is understood: that is the key phrase. Our lately acquired rationalist dialects probably make us quite illiterate in the language of myth.

Atlantis is as mythical as the Land of the Blest, Hy Brazil, Tīr na n-Ōg, the Land of Youth, the Isle of Joy and all the descriptions in which we dress our dreams. In outline, the argument runs that a continent once existed in the place where the Atlantic now is; that it disappeared under the waves, for whatever catastrophic reason, and that the survivors fled east and west. In the west, they formed the higher civilizations of South America; in the east, they became the Sea Peoples who plagued Greece, Egypt and the Mediterranean.

This was the basis of a book written in 1882 by Ignatius Donnelly, an American senator. It was called *Atlantis, the Antediluvian Civilization*. A century later, an Irish author, P.A. O'Siochāin, could still say that Ireland was the last remnant of this civilization and that its peoples were directly related to the lost people of that civilization. The megaliths on the Atlantic coast were the evidence of the outskirts of that territory in the ocean, as were the mighty fortresses on the Aran islands whose builders have never been identified.

The Atlanteans, who are still in tune with the sea, retain a folk memory of their original common heritage: even the Berbers have it. Indeed, these people may have the best claim to be called Atlanteans because part of their home territory is the range of mountains known as the Atlas. They, too, have their Atlantis myth. There is a Sumerian legend of a drowned civilization which Ouzzin, a modern Berber scholar, found contained names that were familiar to him from his own culture. In this legend there is a princess called Tangis, from whose name Tangier is derived. The story goes that she is one day overtaken by a storm at sea and drowned. Her distraught husband begins a search for her which involves attacking an island called Atlantis by means of an underground cavern. The force of his attack causes an earthquake which causes the island to disappear – shades of Thera. The husband becomes a hermit and spends his days sitting on a rock which overlooks the sea, hoping his wife will somehow return. At last the spirit of Tangis calls to him, he is overcome with joy and throws himself into the sea to join her.

The name of the husband intrigued me: it was Lugal – a name that constantly crops up in 'Celtic' mythology. Indeed, London and Lyons are reputed to be named after him. A major pagan feast in Ireland was Lughnasa – the Gaelic name for the month of August. When Lyons was called Lugdunum, it was the scene of one of Caligula's murders. His victim was the last king of Mauretania, home of the Berbers.

No doubt, on the basis of the Lugal story, a scholar could erect a common Sumerian ancestry for both 'Celt' and Berber. I preferred to leave the tangled area of mythology and return to the living evidence. More of this I found in Egypt.

## chapter eleven

St Anthony's monastery is 1600 years old and located in a desolate spot in the hinterland of the Red Sea. A few miles away is the monastery of St Paul. These two foundations are agreed to mark the places where the first anchorites or solitaries lived. Anthony was quite sure he was alone in this wilderness until he accidentally stumbled on Paul who had been there for years before him. From this barren place emerged the saintly madness that fuelled early Irish Christianity and made it unique in the West. This was the principal reason for my presence in Egypt, trying to find pointers which would suggest a direct connection with Ireland. I was, of course, hoping for Arabic and Islamic clues but the Copts impinged on every lead I followed.

I did the normal touristic things: I sailed a felucca on the Nile and confirmed that it had, indeed, the rig of a Conamara pucan; visited the Tutankhamen exhibition in Cairo and noted the Osiris pose of crossed arms which is a particular detail of Irish illuminated manuscripts; saw the gold lunulae or necklets which were common in Ireland over 2000 years ago.

I even found the origin of the shamrock, the national emblem of Ireland. This tiny, three-leaved plant also has a weight of traditional Christian mythology, not to mention theology, surrounding it and is reputed to grow nowhere else but the green isle of Erin. It is said to have been the plant used by Ireland's national apostle to introduce the pagan Irish to the mystery of the Holy Trinity. In the Islamic museum in Cairo I came across some beautifully carved wooden doors which had what looked like three-leaved plants as part of the design. When I enquired about this design the curator said it was something called a 'shamrukh'. Any trefoil plant is called, in Arabic, a 'shamrukh'. In the same museum there were other pieces of wood dated to the third century which bore the imprint of a design in leather, long perished. The designs, to my eyes, were strongly reminiscent of those on some pages of the same Irish illuminated manuscripts.

The phenomenon of desert monasticism was not an invention of Christianity; it had existed long before in ascetic communities like the Katechoi recluses at Memphis in Egypt; the Essenes, writers of the Dead Sea Scrolls, were a Jewish desert community; the Jordan Valley once teemed with saintly eccentrics. Even John the Baptist emerged from a solitary life in the wilderness. The term anchorite comes from the Greek 'anchoresis', meaning departure. Monk simply means, in the same language, 'alone'. The Christian adaptation of this flight to the desert happened in the third and fourth centuries. It sprang mainly from the belief that 'the end of the world was nigh'; the Second Coming was imminent and one should anticipate this by renouncing the world of the flesh. To this end, a variety of saintly retreats developed: living in caves, in holes in the sand, in hollowed-out trees, on the tops of desert stalagmites and many others.

In the desert of the Wadi Natrun, between Cairo and Alexandria, it was estimated that in the early years of this activity there were at least 5000 of these individuals trying to achieve 'solitary' communion with God. It is likely that they were not all either successful or even serious in the attempt to become bona fide saints. The conditions of the peasants of Egypt were so grim that the monastic life must have seemed quite attractive by comparison, particularly when a contemporary of Anthony named Pachomius organized the monks into communities. These embryo monasteries were self-sufficient so an erstwhile peasant stood a good chance of getting fed without the usual hardship.

While not wishing to deprecate the drive for sanctity that must have informed most of these early ascetics, it is also necessary to mention the other incentive to leave the world behind: persecution. The Year of the Martyr in the Coptic Church is 284 AD, when the Emperor Diocletian organized a systematic persecution of Christians. However, even after he stopped, even after the Roman Empire itself adopted Christianity, the persecution of Copts continued. As the Empire became Christian, the Church became imperial.

In the main, these native Egyptians of the Christian persuasion spoke neither Greek nor Latin. They clung to their own Egyptian language, which singled them out from the sophisticated Christians of Alexandria. The Synaxarium of the Coptic Church records considerably more martyrs for the period up to the seventh century when Christianity was dominant than for the years following, when Islam was in charge. This is not so much an indication of the fact that Islam was tolerant, which it was, than of the bitter in-fighting among Christians themselves. By the fifth century, they were divided into Diophysites, Monophysites, Arians, Donatists, Nestorians, Manichaeans and many other competing sects. The Council of Chalcedon, in 451 AD, put the seal on the fate of the Copts and many other Eastern and North African Christians. The latter could not accept the Council's complex formula defining the position of Christ in relation to God; it seemed to diminish the uniqueness of God, His essential One-ness; they, therefore, retreated into what has since been termed a Monophysite position.

A mischievous ex-Benedictine whom I met in Cairo put a different complexion on the matter. Perhaps taking advantage of my Irishness, he claimed that it was because of their ultra-nationalism that the Copts were excluded by the Council of Chalcedon. The finer points of theology were just an excuse. Such nationalism was an attitude that could never fit snugly into the universalist ambitions of a growing Church. There was something vaguely familiar about this thesis.

The survival of the Copts is like a miracle. Rejected by the Orthodox Church for two centuries, until the takeover by Islam made such a rejection academic, they not only preserved their beliefs but also the Egyptian language – the language of the Pharoahs – in which their liturgy is still expressed. They also kept faith with their ancestors by integrating into their liturgical art the very symbols of the Pharoahs: the ankh, symbol of life, was transformed into a Coptic cross; the custom of portraying human bodies with animal heads was directly borrowed from tomb illustrations and incorporated in their icons. The latter device, by the way, is echoed on a stone cross in Monasterboice, Ireland.

Western Christianity lost sight of this unique Church until 1860 when a Presbyterian mission 'discovered' it and tried to convert its members – to Christianity! The Coptic Archbishop of Assiut was understandably irritated: 'We have been living here with Christ for more than 1800 years,' he said. 'How long have you been living with him?' The term Coptic simply means Egyptian. It is derived from the Arabic 'Qubt', a corruption of the Greek 'Aigyptos' which, in turn, is a derivation of the ancient Egyptian 'Hak-ka-Ptah', ie the house of the temple of the spirit of Ptah.

Lest I should give the impression of a Rip Van Winkle sect barely hanging on for life in the deserts of Egypt, I should report that there are as many as seven million members of the Church of Egypt (this is a compromise between the state's estimate of four million and the Copts' estimate of eleven million); that, in Cairo, it has its own 'Vatican', with a pope, schools of theology and fine libraries.

A Coptic deacon mentioned a solid link with Ireland. He knew, he said, that the Copts had influenced early Irish Christianity because at least seven of their monks were recorded as martyrs there. These were the Seven Egyptian Monks noted in the *Martyrology of Tallaght* as having been buried in a place called 'Diseart Ulidh', the Desert of Ulster, which is not known in Ireland. The Copts believed that the monks were buried in Ballymena, which is in Ulster, because one of their known saints is St Mena. However, the real name for Ballymena is – in Gaelic – Baile Meānach which has nothing to do with saints, Coptic or otherwise.

Diseart is a common place-name in Ireland; it means desert and commemorates the early Irish monks' acknowledgement of the influence of North Africa. The number of seven also gives the matter a vagueness because it is a standard figure to indicate perfection or holiness.

In Co Clare there is an old church at a place called Dysert O'Dea. The Gaelic form of this name is Diseart Tōla, meaning Desert of the Flood. Now, if one pronounces this name rapidly, elision causes it to emerge as 'Diseartola' – which is as near as makes no difference to Diseart Ulidh, at least to the tenth-century scribe who first mentioned the Egyptian exiles. In another churchyard in Co Clare, I saw a sculpted stone cross with a strange emblem on it. This featured two sceptres – one the normal shape of a shepherd's crook, the other an odd T-shape. The last time I saw such a staff was in the chapel of St Anthony's in the desert. An old monk was using it for support during the long service. It was also a common feature on the Coptic icons. I further learned it was a standard form of ecclesiastical staff in Ireland up to the ninth century. There are other examples of this carved T-cross still to be found in Ireland. One of the most prominent is on Tory Island, nine miles off the coast of Donegal.

While talking to Father George, my informative Coptic deacon, I noticed a leather cross worn by another priest. It had an ingenious woven pattern, which was very similar, if not identical, to a design carved on a stone called the Fahan Mura, also in Co Donegal. Father George was named after St Girgis who slew Satan in the form of a dragon; this suggested that the Copts had also given England its patron saint. The cumulative effect of discovering odd little details and coincidences like these began to bring into focus an idea I had been harbouring for some time. The development of Irish Christianity has always been something of a puzzle. Nobody knows exactly by which route early monasticism came to the British Isles. Any direct continental evidence that exists gives no hint as to the source of the original contact with Christianity. Oddly enough, the earliest direct references to the existence of Christianity in these remote islands comes from two North Africans – Tertullian and Origen in the third century. The pattern of persecution in the Middle East and North Africa produced a breed of Christian who thought all the 'world' was evil and that one should distance oneself as much as possible from it. The desert is an ideal place for such an exercise but, with 5000 other people having the same intention in the same place, its value as a 'wilderness' decreases. With many of the refugees aspiring more to the security of a monastery than to the true ascetic spirit, the coinage is debased, the atmosphere must become slightly suburban.

Where could the true believers go? They were accustomed to seeking oases, the islands of the desert. Why not even more inaccessible islands, those of the sea? The furthest place you can go in the world is the edge of that world. The Greeks had described a Holy Isle. Ptolemy the Alexandrian had charted it. The Carthaginians had, it was believed, visited it. The Ancient World had, as we have seen, many beliefs about places called the Fortunate Isles in the far west, a paradise beyond the setting sun, the Continent of Kronos, Ogygia, the Garden of the Hesperides, Atlantis etc. But, more important, there were legends of a northern sea called Marimorusa, ie mare mortuum, the sea of the dead. The culture of the anchorite aimed at being 'dead' to the world. In the light of their belief that the world was inherently evil, and the sooner they were shut of it the better, a sea of the dead must seem highly appropriate.

Coptic and Syrian refugees are known to have 'relocated' in quite substantial numbers in southern Gaul. They formed a distinct community there in the fourth and fifth centuries. Their existence must have been precarious, representing a branch of Christianity deemed heretical by both eastern and western orthodoxies.

The early form that this religion took in Ireland appears to have been much closer to the desert solitaries. The earliest monastic settlements were tiny, crude, scattered and numerous – more like shrines than monasteries. The Skelligs Rock – eight miles from the coast of Kerry – is sheer enough, rugged enough, cruel enough to satisfy the most masochistic ambitions of any anchorite. The stone huts of these ascetics still survive on the rocks. The early literature endlessly quotes examples of such anchorites in remote places like the Skelligs. Like Egyptian monasticism, which was a revolt against ecclesiastical organization and the episcopal system, the early Irish Church had a base firmly rooted in the tribe. A leader, or 'abbot' could inherit his role from his father, and bishops were under his thumb. But even this was a later development than the initial phenomenon of the solitaries.

It is worth recalling the edicts of Theodosius in the fourth century when he clamped down on movement into and out of the Empire. This may have had as much application in the religious as in the commercial sphere. The Copts and many other North African Christians were 'outside the pale'. That is why most of the Coptic missionary activity that is recorded was in a southerly direction, in Nubia and Ethiopia, in areas avoided by Greek and Roman.

I have already suggested that the tightening of restrictions on travel through the now-Christian Empire must have produced a stimulus to travel on its borders. It has also been shown that sea travel was a normal way of covering large distances. I saw no reason why the phenomenon known as early Irish Christianity should not have come directly from North Africa, bypassing continental Europe and only making 'pit-stops' along the Atlantic coasts.

While in Cairo I simply wandered the streets, keeping my eyes and ears open. That was how I noticed some women with a 'lozenge' or diamond-shaped mark on their foreheads. These marks reminded me that the Berber practice of tattooing was universal throughout North Africa. The more traditional Copts had a cross tattooed on their wrists. Those who pretended to sophistication, and did not wear this sign of faith, explained that 'they carried the cross in their hearts'.

The Irish monks, known as wanderers for Christ, are also reputed to have used tattooing.

They certainly painted their eyelids, as is recorded in a manuscript in St Gall, Switzerland. Where did they get this custom which, along with their unorthodox appearance, so irritated the clerical authorities on the Continent? Pope Celestine wrote on the danger of appointing 'wanderers and strangers' to local episcopal office: 'They who have not grown up in the Church, act contrary to the Church's usage . . . coming from other customs . . . clad in a cloak with a girdle round their loins.' He may have been talking about the Irish; they were certainly unorthodox, if not heretical. The disputes over hair-styles and the date of Easter were so vehement at the Synod of Whitby in 664 AD that the Northern Irish Christians decamped back to Iona in Scotland and thence to Ireland.

The efforts to integrate this awkward thing called 'early Irish Christianity' into a respectable European mould have been energetic. They range from the explanation that the Coptic/Syrian influence in Gaul accounts for its idiosyncrasies, to the possibility that St Patrick himself brought back oriental touches from the Egyptian-influenced monastery of Lerins, off the south coast of Gaul.

St Patrick was British, which coincided with the belief that all the efforts to civilize the Irish came from that quarter. There is no written mention of the saint until the seventh century, two hundred years after his supposed conversion of the Irish. It is very odd that he is not mentioned at all by prominent scribes like Gildas, Bede, Adamnān or Columbanus. The supposed date of his arrival, 432 AD, is clearly a 'mythological' number.

In the Icelandic sagas, Valhalla has 540 doors through each of which 800 warriors pass. Multiply the two figures and the result is 432,000. In the Chaldean legends of Babylon, the interval between the building of the first city, Kish, and the disaster of the Flood is also 432,000 years. Astronomically, the number of years in one complete cycle of the procession of the equinoxes is 25,920. If that is divided by 60 – the basic multiple of the most ancient Mesopotamian mathematical system – the answer is 432. Even in the Puranas, old Indian epics, there is a great cycle referred to as the Day of Brahma which is estimated at 432,000 years. This date, 432 AD, appears to have been chosen for its metaphysical and allegorical dimension, to attach some form of 'profundity' to what was simply a clerical takeover of Irish history. Just as the scribes of the early Middle Ages fitted the pagan Irish tradition into a classical chronology, so also must they have assigned a cosmological number like 432 as a date to a significant event, ie the alleged coming of Christianity in the form of St Patrick. Fortunately, we know that there were Christians in Ireland before him, if he existed at all. He was sent 'to those Irish believing in Christ'. The story of Patrick driving the snakes from Ireland is also mythical: there never were snakes in Ireland. It is not many years since Professor O Rahilly suggested that there were two St Patricks. This would certainly satisfy those Egyptians and Lebanese who believe that they each sent a St Patrick to Ireland.

As I emphasized before, it is better to try to understand the meaning of a myth than to dismiss it altogether. The 'shamrukh' is an eastern word – in fact, its first mention in relation to Ireland was written in the twelfth century, the period of the Crusades. Its use as a teaching device by Patrick – to explain the three-in-one concept of the Trinity – may be significant because this 'Trinity' was precisely the point of friction between 'orthodox' Christianity and the schismatic Copts, Syrians and all the other Monophysite religions.

The story of the snakes is also so bizarre that it, too, must have a meaning. It happens that in the

North Africa of this early period there was a Christian sect called the Ophites or Naasenes who worshipped God in the form of a serpent. This was because they believed the god defined by their orthodox enemies and persecutors must be evil; consequently, that god's enemy – the serpent – must be the real God. Patrick's reputed success with the snakes is very likely a rich metaphor to illustrate the ultimate triumph of orthodoxy over a pre-existing form of Christianity in Ireland which consisted of sects like the Ophites. However, this triumph was not totally achieved until the twelfth century when, as mentioned before, the Normans arrived to sort out the Irish.

It appeared, to me, that the conventional account of early Irish Christianity as a slightly bizarre offshoot of respectable European orthodoxy might have been an invention of this late period. If the clerical scribes could 'synchronize' pagan history with classical history, similarly the early development of the religion on this island was brought into line with an idealized account of the Great Western Church.

This is not simply wild speculation. Starting from first principles, there is the idea that Gordon Childe outlined in 1958 – that the activities of 'Celtic' saints might be compared to the spread of megalithic tombs in Western Europe. As he maintained that the idea for these tombs emanated from the Eastern Mediterranean and spread west, through the Straits of Gibraltar and up the Atlantic coasts, I took this as a supportive analogy. The ancient wine routes from the Mediterranean to the north were presumably not disrupted by theological squabbles. It would explain the pieces of pottery found in Garranes, Co Cork, as well as Cornwall, which were identified as having come directly from Alexandria in Egypt. It would explain a cache of 'pearls' found quite recently in a grave at

Plouhinec – not far from the megaliths of Morbihan in Brittany – which were identified as Egyptian and dated to the fourth century, the period when persecution was a strong motive for travelling. It would explain the Book of Adam and Eve composed in Egypt in about the fifth century and known in no country in Europe except Ireland, where it became Saltair na Rann.

In Cairo, I met a journalist – he also happened to be a Jesuit priest – who had studied the relationship between the Copts and the 'Celts' for seventeen years. He was convinced there were solid grounds for suggesting such a connection. He based his opinion not only on liturgical and monastic similarities but on the semi-pagan rituals that still underlie many of these practices. He instanced the processions for the dead in Brittany (of which he was a native) and those in the Egyptian deserts which also took place in November.

In Egypt, also, I had long conversations with a musicologist who had spent nearly fifty years living in that country. I played to her a tape-recording of the sean-nōs singing of Conamara. She listened attentively and then said its pentatonic form was not Arabic but was characteristic of Nubian singing and of the African countries in general. But could such a musical form have travelled all the way to the west of Ireland? She by no means dismissed the idea and, in fact, mentioned an example that Bela Bartók had discovered, of the transmission of music over many miles and many years. He had found a community in the Caucasus who had emigrated from Hungary 600 years previously but who still retained the precise melodies and words they had brought with them from the home country. I was so pleased to hear this that I went to a Nubian wedding to celebrate. Then I heard the amazing sound of the 'zagharit' –

the fierce, tongue-rolling yodel of the women. I knew that this could be experienced in any country of North Africa: another example of how a distinctive vocal expression can be shared by people a thousand miles apart. Bearing in mind the monks of the desert of Egypt, I thought of what a Conamara sean-nōs singer had told me about the origin of her music: she said the old folk thought it came from 'the monks'.

To generalize, the structure and ethos of the early Irish Church is so impregnated with Eastern and North African characteristics, that to attribute it to second-hand influences is begging too many questions. Once again I must invoke the maritime argument and the feasibility of influence along the Atlantic seaways. The Copts of Egypt, because they are living evidence of similarity, are an obvious group on which to base this possibility.

Carthage, with its long history – legendary or not – of contact with the British Isles was also a prime locus of possibility. It was here that the major heresy of Donatism grew. Like the Copts, the Carthaginian Christians were completely integrated with their local cultures and languages. The Carthaginians were Punic and Berber. They were not just a minor tributary to the mainstream of Christianity, nor were they a minor sect. One of their bishops, Timgad, left the largest and finest cathedral in North Africa. The history of Carthaginian wars with the pagan Roman Empire – the Punic Wars – was not forgotten. In time, they spilled over into a mistrust of the Imperial Roman Church. These people were anti-authoritarian, independent-minded and puritan. They thought that the Church's alliance with the Empire was disastrous in that it became too worldly. Christianity had come to Carthage early in the second century and retained an early idealism which refused to compromise with a world seen as evil.

They were highly organized, with as many as five hundred bishops on whom they kept a tight rein, ever watchful for signs of arrogance or decadence. They coined the title 'Communion of Saints' for themselves, a title later taken over by the Imperial Church.

It was their obsession with personal perfection that started the row. The Carthaginians maintained that if a bishop was a sinner – particularly if during earlier persecutions he had collaborated with the then pagan Empire – it invalidated his sacramental role. Things came to a head when eighty Numidian bishops objected to the appointment of Caecilian as Bishop of Carthage on the grounds that the celebrant of the rite was a 'sinner'. They appointed a man named Donatus in his stead. The resulting conflict expressed itself in a war between sophisticated, urbanized, Christians – the liberals of those days – and the nationalistic, indigenous people. The Emperor Constantine naturally supported the former who represented the Roman point of view.

Persecution of the native Church lasted for the next sixty years. Orthodoxy had the weight of the secular Empire on its side but the Carthaginians were well organized and were fighting on their home territory. They even developed private armies of 'circumcelliones' who carried cudgels to make sure their own bishops were not tempted to capitulate on the issues. I was interested to learn that absentee Roman landlords here maintained large estates – a legacy of the original conquerors of Hannibal, the destroyers of the original Carthage. The Donatists became a kind of guerrilla force who made sorties against these estates.

The Orthodox Church, in alliance with the physical might of the Empire, conducted a campaign both political and physical to destroy the Donatists. A number of Councils was held ostensibly to try to resolve the dispute. But, in the end, Donatus was excommunicated, his followers more intensively persecuted. The chief architect of this victory was also a North African – a man born in Algeria of a mother called Monika and a father called, interestingly, Patrick. He was the famous St Augustine of Hippo – a man described as 'the dark genius of Imperial Christianity, the fabricator of the mediaeval mentality'. For the first thirty years of even this famous saint's life, he belonged to a heretical sect called the Manichees. But that, apparently, was not remarkable in a man of his family in those early years of Christianity.

Paul Johnson describes the end of Donatism:

> Even after a long bout of imperial persecution, inspired by Augustine, the Donatists were still able to produce nearly 300 bishops for the final attempt at compromise at Carthage in 411. Thereafter in the course of two decades, before the Vandals overran the littoral, the back of the Donatist church was broken by force. Its upperclass supporters joined the establishment. Many of its rank and file were driven into outlawry and brigandage. There were many case of mass suicide.

North Africa seemed to be the last refuge of the ancient traditions of asceticism, non-conformism and general independence of mind. Rome and Constantinople became 'orthodox' and imperial; North Africa stayed nationalist and became schismatic. It sounded, to me, like a perfect recipe for what I had learned of the early Irish Church. What became of all these North Africans, with their passionate religious beliefs? They could not all have conformed to the Augustinian idea of total religious uniformity. The majority which stayed in North Africa must have submitted very reluctantly. The ease with which Islam took over two centuries later – it had no priests, no pope, just a clear belief in one God – shows that. But what of those who refused to serve? Is it not likely they would have searched for a place beyond the reach of the Imperial Church, a place well known by reputation, a place the Roman Empire had never touched: Ireland? When the Irish missionaries began to spread their wings and travel abroad, when Brendan and the others began their voyaging, there was no nervousness about long sea trips. What is solely in question is the length of the voyage they undertook to get here in the first place.

What I hope to have shown is that a voyage from North Africa to these northern islands in those awful early centuries of religious strife and persecution must have seemed, not a frightening prospect, but a delightful chance of escape. There actually existed a green and pleasant land free of interminable theological quarrels, of rapacious bishops, of an increasingly bureaucratic – and corrupt – Church. One did not have to travel overland a thousand miles through European territories where in one you were in danger if you were an Arian, in another you were accused of Donatism, or Montanism, or Manichaeanism, or Nestorianism, or even Pelagianism – any of the hundred and one 'heresies' which, in fact, you might actually be proud to profess.

Indeed, when you read of these many 'heresies', you wonder on what narrow ground could orthodoxy possibly reside. In the course of my researches I learned that heresy was not a description of an objectionable innovation. It was precisely the opposite. A Church adapting to political reality in its many forms was forced to drop some ancient practices adopted for the time being from older religions. It was mainly these older practices and beliefs, retained by some Christians, that were condemned as heretical. In the year 390 AD, there were 156 distinct 'heresies' in full flight. In the fifth century, there were at least a hundred official Church statutes in opposition to such deviances. So much for the idea of monolithic, united Christianity.

These are incidental to my main interest: the possibility that the early Irish Church owed little to continental Europe – that, in fact, the reverse was true; that this religion travelled by a circular route – following the earlier trading routes – westwards along the Mediterranean, up the Atlantic coasts, hibernating in Ireland for a while, then moving onwards through Scotland and England into Europe.

It was in the matter of art that I found more support for this idea.

# chapter twelve

For years Westerners with fat wallets had collected Coptic books and textiles. Impoverished monks had co-operated reluctantly. The best examples were reputed to be in New York but I thought I would rather see one of these books in a natural context, the desert Monastery of St Macarius in Wadi Natrun. In that way I might get an inkling of the holy intensity that enabled men more than a thousand years ago meticulously to copy out sacred texts and adorn them with designs derived from a rich Middle Eastern tradition of art. I was hoping to find in these illuminated books some evidence that they might have been produced antecedent to the Books of Kells and Durrow in Ireland.

The earliest that Father Johann could show me was a Book of the Office, called the 'Katameros' which was made in 1052! The Irish books were designed in the seventh and eighth centuries. However, I did learn that the physical age of such books was no measure of the antiquity of the designs. When a monastic scribe was copying a book, his belief that it was the word of God made him fanatically careful to reproduce it precisely. An Irish scribe put it like this: 'I beseech all those who may wish to copy these books, nay more, I adjure them through Christ the judge of all the ages, that after careful copying, they compare them with the exemplar from which they have written and emend them with utmost care.'

Allowing for variations in graphic skill, the designs would have followed a similar pattern, so that one executed in the tenth century could easily be a close representation of a design conceived centuries before. This was actually demonstrated to me by an Assyrian doctor in Gloucester, England. Dr Lazar Lazar had learned a technique from his father, who had, in turn, learned it from his father. The doctor sat at his kitchen table and drew a pattern of dots which he then connected with lines and produced a design identical to that which I had seen in Father Johann's books. The function of the dots was to ensure that the designs could be transmitted almost mechanically by people of little natural artistic skill. The same technique was used in some of the more prosaic designs of the Irish books.

The fact that these Syriac and Coptic designs had lost much of their original dynamism did not take away from the fact that some of their elements were echoed in the Irish books. The designs I saw in Egypt, and later in the Chester Beatty Library, were complex and beautiful but there was something inert about them, as if frozen in time. They did not, like the Irish designs, 'move in their stillness'. They had little of the life and flow of the Books of Kells and Durrow – nor of the Koranic designs which have been likened to them. But then, I thought, what else could one expect from a Church like the Coptic which had literally been isolated for more than a thousand years; in order to preserve its identity it would have had to retreat into repetition and conservatism.

Further, it was obvious that when a schismatic Church produced such books, they were odious to the Orthodox authorities; the first casualties of persecution would have been such books. Who knows how many thousands of Coptic and Syriac manuscripts were destroyed by Rome and Constantinople, even by Islam when it arrived. Fortunately, there is some evidence that this art of book illumination was once alive and vibrant. It exists in some detail in the Syriac Gospels in the Chester

Beatty Library and also in the Glazier collection in New York. In fact, in the Harklean version of the Syriac Gospels in Dublin, which is a tenth-century copy of a seventh-century book, there are resemblances to the Irish designs. At the bottom of many pages is a tiny design of interlace which I would at one time have described as 'Celtic'. One cartoon of a fisherman has the same sense of humour that one finds in Kells. In the Glazier collection there is a design, made no later than the fifth century, which uses a broad yellow and red interlace design which is unmistakably related to a carpet page in the Book of Durrow – a book produced at least a century later.

The similarities between Irish and Eastern illuminated manuscripts are both stylistic and concrete. Early Christian pictures of the Virgin and Christ-child depict the Adoration of the Magi: the Virgin is shown holding the Christ-child facing outwards, presenting him to the Wise Men. This image – so often found on sarcophagi from early Christian Rome – is quite distinct from the Kells' Virgin and Christ-child in which the Virgin holds the Christ-child facing inwards as if nursing him: the Magi are absent. This image is an important development in Christian art as it shows the Virgin and the Christ-child outside a scriptural context – the picture is an icon not an illustration to accompany part of the Gospel. The Virgin and Christ-child is the only illuminated page in the Book of Kells which does not serve as an illustration to the narrative.

The change from narrative to iconic illumination may well have taken place in Egypt where the Coptic Church was influenced by the Pharonic cult of Isis. The image of Isis suckling Horus is frequently found, the Divine Goddess is represented with human attributes. This image converts to Christian tradition easily – representing the

Queen of Heaven and showing maternal affection as the earthly mother of Jesus. The legacy of the Isis image provides a starting point for the art of the Virgin: it is interesting to note that the Christ-child in the Kells' illumination does not have a halo, the focus is on the figure of the Virgin. This is more appropriate to Isis and Horus, where the mother is the superior figure, than to Mary and Jesus where the Child is more important.

The Kells' Virgin is flanked by four angels; the lower right angel carries a split foliate staff, the other angels each carry a flabellum – an Eastern instrument for keeping flies away from the communion table. The archangels Michael, Gabriel, Raphael and Uriel are especially honoured by the Coptic Church but the Kells' Virgin is unique in being flanked by four angels – in the monastic cycle at Saggara, there are two angels beneath the Virgin and two local saints above. There are four angels flanking Christ in the Ascension scene in the Syriac Rabbula Gospels (dated 586) and again in the Ascension icon from the monastery of St Catherine, Sinai.

There was one fascinating piece of information about the Kells and Durrow books which encouraged me to seek further analogies with North Africa. It related to the colouring techniques used. Natural pigments and dyes were only available at the time of their creation. The colour red in both books is derived from red lead mixed with a substance called 'kermes' which, it transpires, was made from the pregnant body of a Mediterranean insect called the Kermococcus vermilio. Purples, mauves and maroons were derived from a plant called Crozophora tinctoria – also from the Mediterranean. To add an exotic touch, shades of blue were reputed to derive from lapis lazuli which came from mines in the foothills of the Himalayas!

In my conversation with Father Johann, I mentioned the similarity between the designs on his books and Islamic manuscripts I had previously seen. In view of the fact that the books in his custody were mainly dated later than, for instance, the Ibn Bawwab Koran in the Chester Beatty, I innocently wondered if the Copts might not have learned from the Muslims. He handled my ignorance gently, pointing out that the Arabs who emerged from the desert might have had great faith and a wonderful oral tradition but they had little art and less literature. They had learned from the peoples they conquered. These included the Egyptians who had a proven record in art and – in the case of the Copts – textiles.

Book illumination was developed in the Middle East and particularly Persia, long before Christianity came to these islands. The second fact was that, although the earlier illuminations such as in Durrow are non-representational and are thus in the iconoclastic tradition of early Eastern Christianity (and Islam), very soon other influences creep in. There are Byzantine faces and bodies, Viking animals which are cleverly integrated into the native Irish tradition. The latter is undoubtedly what gives these designs their energy and is without doubt the most striking characteristic. The other features are evidence of an openness to widespread influences from as far as Constantinople and Scandinavia but the Irish design can be traced back through centuries before Kells and Durrow and is a clear argument that these books were produced by scholars and scribes trained in the island.

In teasing out the provenance of the individual design elements there is always a temptation to ignore the larger question: what inspired this relatively sudden explosion of talent in the island, an event not parensled in Europe? There must have been a desperate ideal which fused these disparate elements together into what Françoise Henry has described as 'the most satisfying and most perfect form of non-representational art which Europe has ever known'.

The art developed and flourished in a place normally considered to be on the periphery of civilized human affairs but which, on this evidence, clearly was not. It was later transmitted to Europe by the wandering monks; examples can be found in Irish-founded monasteries throughout the Continent. It is a graphic illustration of the process of culture-spread, the model of circular diffusion which had become very real to me: seaborne, carried by people outside the control of centralized religions or Empires, in a constant traffic on the edges of Europe, moving ideas and artefacts along the coasts and islands of the Mediterranean, the Atlantic and the North Sea, occasionally taking root and blossoming in the most unlikely places, later to expand into darkest Europe.

One such unlikely place is the Aran Islands, off the west coast of Ireland. I have detailed the strange observations of blood-group specialists in connection with these islands. Now I came across another odd connection with Coptic Egypt. The people of Aran are famous for the unusual quality of knitted garments produced there. There is now a small industry on the middle island, Inis Meāin, which has developed this home craft into a major exporting business. But the women of these islands still knit at home and create the fine designs which have made this knitting noteworthy. The patterns are memorized and transmitted to the children who continue the tradition. Each woman has her own repertoire of designs. Traditionally, if an islander was drowned, the most reliable means of identification was the sweater he was wearing.

When I was initially speculating on Conamara, its music, its sailing tradition and matters related to it, the phenomenon of the Aran knitting patterns – just a few miles away – constantly nagged at me. I learned that knitting was originally a male occupation, developed by sailors on long voyages and by fishermen waiting for the fish to bite: again, the maritime dimension. It was natural that seafarers should have evolved a 'cable stitch'; but what kind of sailors could have developed the other more elaborate patterns: the 'diamond', the 'trellis', the 'zig-zag', the 'tree of life', the 'Trinity' stitch, the 'honeycomb', the 'spoon' stitch? One could imagine a hardy island people producing some functional pattern as they did in Jersey and Guernsey but these Aran ideas were complex, luxuriant: a celebration. They had to be a manifestation of more than basic needs; perhaps there was a more profound, even religious, motivation? This would fit the title: Aran of the Saints. There was plenty of evidence on the islands for a thriving religious community a thousand years before. I did not believe the customary explanation of these monastic remains, that they had been built by monks who were drop-outs from larger foundations on the mainland. It was too much like the landlubber thesis of diffusion, that everything had to originate on a mainland. What was to stop monks coming directly from the south, by sea?

These early speculations of mine received a stimulus when I met a man called Heinz Edgar Kiewe – a specialist in, of all things, knitting. He had even written the definitive *The Sacred History of Knitting* in which he maintained that the islanders of Aran had received their design inspiration from the Coptic monks! Those knitting patterns were, according to him, an illiterate people's way of expressing profound religious ideas. Kiewe gave credit to the indigenous flair for 'Celtic' design but he maintained that the order, the way in which these native designs achieved their formal Christian expression – even in the Book of Kells, came from the Copts.

'Folklorists have a habit,' he said, 'of becoming too enthusiastic about insular tradition. Since they usually live in big towns and take the importance of political geography too seriously, they often mix up nationalism with the migration of symbols and designs. The latter are usually inspired by faith and superstition rather than by local genius. Abstract folk designs of Europe generally came with the pilgrims, the missionaries, the pirates and/or favourable trade winds to the northern countries from the Eastern Mediterranean where the three great religions were born.'

Kiewe first encountered the Aran designs in Dublin and was amazed by their complexity. He sent one sweater to a knitting specialist in London who thought the garment was a 'sampler', a virtuoso display of all the stitches available. At that time there was only one interlace pattern in the knitting vocabulary of the British Isles; this was the cable stitch used by the Jersey and Guernsey islanders. The Aran sweater far exceeded these in the profusion of its patterns.

Heinz Edgar Kiewe was not only a technician in this area; he had developed a philosophy about the simple craft which seemed to summarize the permanent tension between the classical trappings of the Great Church and the tenacious witness of an early, more humble Christianity: 'Graeco-Roman classical art became the golden measure for a millennium,' he said, 'but craft which furthers the continuity of ancient cosmopolitan, abstract symbols, lingers on, not in urban regions but rather along the coasts, on the isles, with the sailors of the seven seas.'

He was suitably sceptical about the nineteenth-century revival of romantic interest in folk art but, at the same time, was quite definite about the Aran islanders' knitting skills and their religious origin: 'The beginnings of civilization of craft on the islands was in the hands of the monks who brought with them to the North patterns of the Coptic designs, with which they created formal abstract interlace patterns in their illuminated bibles, missals, crosses, croziers and carved stone crosses. No doubt the local population toiled with the monks in building, maintaining and beautifying the church and were thus inspired by the character of style which in the eighth century displays three elements in Irish art: Coptic, Anglo-Saxon and native Irish.'

When I met Mr Kiewe in his textile sop in Oxford, he decided that he had been too generous to the Anglo-Saxons and he removed the reference to them. He showed the relationship between the broad ribbon interlace of the Book of Durrow – 'derived almost certainly from Coptic sources', and the Aran pattern which he called the 'caduceus', the intertwining 'Jacob's Ladder' which he said originated in the signs of Hermes and Mercury, originally the symbol of Healing. He concluded: 'It is true that the Aran patterns belong . . . to the international faith of the Gospel in all lands, to the apostles, the missionaries and the pilgrims who carried with them as signs of the Holy Land some scrap of textile as an amulet – a thing easily carried, easily hidden . . . the Aran patterns . . . are symbols of the divine geometrical speculations of the Near East.'

The people of the Aran Islands retain a skill which may link them with the genius of design in Ireland in the seventh and eighth centuries, as well as with the early Christianity of Egypt and North Africa. In fact, Kiewe has found an illustration in the Book of Kells which he is convinced supports his ideas. It is usually referred to as 'Daniel feeding the Dragon' but Kiewe sees in it a figure wearing a knitted garment. It took years for the expert Françoise Henry to confirm his opinion that it was, indeed, a figure wearing 'a sort of tightly fitting knitted costume'. As a footnote, I might mention one item of apparel on the islands: this is the 'crios', a hand-woven, multi-coloured sash made of wool. The word itself is derived from 'Crīosdaī', Christian in Gaelic. The only other place I have heard of this particular design is in Portugal, also worn by fishermen, also on the Atlantic seaways.

The earliest Irish book in existence, which begins to experiment with graphic embellishment, is the 'Cathach' attributed to the sixth century. It is a famous book in that the first ruling on the law of copyright was made on its behalf. A scribe who had copied the book without permission refused to hand over the copy. A saint was called on to arbitrate and he pronounced judgement thus: 'To every cow its calf and to every book its copy.' In the Cathach one finds the first example of a distinctive Irish script, usually called the 'Celtic' half-uncial. Here is the first expression of the tendency to produce elaborate initial letters which is developed wonderfully in the Books of Kells and Durrow. I had these initial letters in mind as I searched through the Syriac and Coptic books in the Chester Beatty Library, among them three little Coptic books described as 'the best preserved vellum books of such an early date – 6th century – that have been discovered in Egypt'. They were called the Saqquara manuscripts. In them I found initial letters which, in my view, could easily have been drawn by the monk who wrote the Cathach.

Gradually, I learned about other similarities between the Coptic and the Irish books. They both had the same method of binding the pages; they both used dots liberally to outline figures; they only partially completed the framing of some of their designs; their use of red, yellow and green coincided closely; a lozenge design on the Virgin and Child in the Kells' Book was popular with the Copts – it may have had something to do with the tattoo I had noted on the faces of women in Egypt. The Irish use of these features was unique in Western Europe. Once more it seemed that this island was directly in touch – through a maverick Church – with North Africa.

Before I left Egypt I found one other similarity, this time secular. In a public park in Cairo I came across a group of musicians and dancers who were performing a strange ritual. Two men faced each other like Robin Hood and Little John, each wielding a long wooden staff with which they seemed to be trying to decapitate the other. In their long, flowing djellabas they danced round each other, clashing their staffs in rhythm with the drums and pipes. It was obviously a ritual enactment of battle. This stick dance is performed throughout North Africa and Conor Cruise O'Brien has remarked on its similarity to an Irish custom performed by 'mummers'.

The Wexford Mummers dress in a kind of bishop's garb and face each other in a line. They use shorter sticks than the Egyptians and produce a greater noise, accompanied by the fiddles and flutes of traditional Irish music. It is also a ritual of battle – the military ranks in contrast with the man-to-man combat suggested by the North Africans – but it has definite religious overtones. It so happens that the term 'mummer' comes from the term 'Mohammedan', itself a pejorative description used by Westerners to describe the religion of Islam. 'Mummery' is consequently defined in Western dictionaries as 'an absurd, superstitious rite'. It perfectly sums up the traditional Christian,

Western attitude to rival religions.

The Wexford Mummers are unconsciously mimicking the stick dance of North Africa and probably, thereby, commemorating the sorry history of clashes between Christians and Muslims.

# chapter thirteen

The Sheela na Gig figures have been described in various ways: 'the Irish Goddess of Creation': 'an obscene female figure of uncertain significance'; 'a fertility figure, usually with legs apart'; finally, 'a female exhibitionist figure – one of the many representations of lust in Romanesque carving'. Well over one hundred of these extraordinary stone figures have been found in Ireland. The carvings are quite explicit in that the entire attention of the observer is directed at the female genitals. They owe nothing to classical ideas of beauty, indeed, seem to go out of their way to be crude. There is no doubt that the Sheela na Gigs are somehow associated with religion because they have been found built into the walls of churches and convents as well as castles. Their very crudeness suggests that hundreds more may have been the casualties of righteous assaults by puritans, Victorians and clergymen. The finest and the most explicit are held in the basement of the National Museum in Dublin. They have never been exhibited to the public – the Sheela na Gigs are an embarrassment. How can they be fitted into the chaste image of the Ireland of Saints and Scholars where, according to standard hagiography, the Irish saint

lived in a hole in the wall,
a life of ferocious austerity.
He suffered from violent gall
and on women he looked with asperity.

One can imagine the thoughts of Victorian

antiquarians when they first encountered these figures. In some of their sketches they tried to diminish the sexual explicitness, in others they deliberately altered the position of limbs to turn the figures into innocuous contortionists. That they mentioned the Sheelas at all is an indication of the figures' widespread existence; they could not be totally ignored. The stone carvings are found in a broad swathe stretching from Co Louth in the east to Kerry in the south-west, with the greatest concentration in Offaly – near the River Shannon – and in Tipperary, near the River Suir.

The first general point that can be made is that they come from an age when sexual prudery was not the norm in Ireland. Actually to imagine such an age is difficult, so deep has been the impact of Jansenism and other narrow continental ideas on the island. The destruction of the Gaelic culture in the seventeenth century which was bawdily healthy – as evidenced by Brian Merriman's epic *The Midnight Court* – opened the doors to puritanism, pessimism and anti-intellectualism. To me, at least, it was a delighted shock when I first encountered the Sheelas in 1975. In a country which had made itself a laughing stock with its censorship laws, it was stunning to discover that the Irish had been producing 'erotic' carvings at least 700 years ago.

The reason the Sheelas could be dated at least as early as that was that some of the churches and castles into which they were incorporated were built in the twelfth century. There is now a strong tendency to attribute their first appearance to this period of Anglo-Norman influence: the Sheelas were part of a European development of exhibitionist carvings which were commonplace on the pilgrim routes to places like Santiago de Campostella. The object of these carvings was to warn the pious away from occasions of lust. They featured angels, devils, men and women in the most imaginative possible range of acrobatic positions. Indeed, what strikes one is the sheer 'dirty-mindedness' of the mediaeval carvers. In the most splendid Gothic and Romanesque cathedrals you have an impressive array of male and female anal exhibition, phallic display, genital assault, beard-pulling (a euphemism), androgyny, breast display – all of the practices which we associate with pornography. It is possible that these activities reflected the amusements of the ordinary people of the time, including clerics, and which a mediaeval Church – inspired by St Augustine – wished to eradicate. Pilgrims on their way to amend their lives might wish to have one last sinful fling on the long and hard road to the holy shrines. All along the routes prostitution was big business. The obscene carvings were the antidote, a means of trying to frighten people into church. In placing the Sheela na Gigs in this continental context – as writers like Jorgen Andersen and Anthony Weir have brilliantly attempted – they have left me with a few loose ends.

The first is the assumption that the carvings all date from the twelfth century onwards. It is impossible to date stone as a material; a carving made yesterday will have much the same date as a stone taken from the same quarry a million years ago. The only loose dating methods are stylistic and typological, ie locating the stone in a particular historical context, one that has a known date. Because of the provenance of Sheelas in buildings of the Anglo-Norman period and later, it is assumed they were carved not earlier than that period. A Sheela functioning as a corner stone in a building was clearly put there when the building was first erected. But the carvings in the National Museum, for instance, are on stones so awkwardly shaped that it is hard to imagine them fitting comfortably into any well-built structure.

It is a fact that examples of Sheela na Gigs, so widespread in Ireland, are – in this precise form – quite scarce in Britain and Europe. The idea of exhibitionism certainly exists, and in a very definite style, but the specific unwieldiness of the female imagery of the Sheela seems to be a speciality of Ireland. Even their crudeness cannot be used as evidence of a lack of stone-carving skill on the island; the brilliance of Irish stone crosses is enough testimony to a fine tradition of stonemen. The occasional suggestion that the crude Sheelas are a poor insular attempt to imitate the custom of fine exhibitionist carving on the Continent is – at least from the point of view of craft – a libel. But, even allowing for such a thesis; even if Irish carvers were slavishly copying a continental example, is it likely that they would have confined themselves almost exclusively to this grotesque female form? Rarely is there an example of the continental acrobatics, rarely a decent phallus. The daring range of imagery listed earlier does not find its expression widely in Ireland. The Sheela stands almost alone. Admittedly, it is easier to destroy a phallic figure's distinctiveness than that of a Sheela. But such phallic figures are rare in Ireland in contrast to Britain or Europe where the Roman Empire ensured widespread familiarity with the cult of Priapus. I found a fine example of such a phallic figure in a tiny museum attached to Margam Abbey in South Wales.

One positive feature of the Anglo-Normans who came to Ireland was that, unlike subsequent conquerors, they integrated so well with the natives that eventually they adopted the Gaelic language and became 'more Irish than the Irish themselves'. This suggests that they may have adopted some of the local customs also. What if the natives already practised the custom of erecting a talisman in the form of a female figure on their buildings? What if, when the newcomers went to build their keeps and castles, they sensibly used the stones of ruined buildings – including those already fashioned into Sheelas – quite a practical custom. The Sheela na Gigs have been found in so many different situations – in castles, churches, fields, streams, used as gateposts, parts of stone walls – there is no way of knowing how ancient some of them might be. Their widespread distribution throughout the island points to an integration with the tradition of the people, a normality of usage, that counters the idea of a passing fashion imported from the Continent.

One could actually turn the argument upside down. Some centuries before the period usually associated with the Sheelas, Irish monks were in part responsible for the revival of learning in Europe. Could one not argue that, along with their scholarship, they brought an exotic concept of the role of the female in religion to the Continent? The Irish monks were not uniformly celibate. That odd restriction was not enforced in Ireland until many centuries afterwards. What if these wanderers also brought with them to Europe the germ of an idea which the mediaeval Church would later incorporate into its gruesome inconography. A pointer to this might be one of the best examples of the Sheela in Britain, that in Kilpeck Church, Hereford. It is reputed to have been carved by Irish craftsmen.

In Ptolemaic Egypt, women in childbirth had the habit of keeping by their sides a female figurine called a Baubo. It had the same posture as a Sheela. Its precise function is unknown but as it was a well-fleshed figure it is assumed to have some fertility connotations. I enquired about such a figure in every museum in Cairo but nobody had ever heard of it. This must have been partly because no such daring figure would have a place in Islam; perhaps, also, because German scholars at the turn of the century brought many of the available figurines home with them: the best examples are in Berlin. For me, the Baubo clarified one aspect of the Sheela na Gig. The latter is usually a fairly emaciated figure. The breasts are flat or non-existent. The figure is the exact reverse of what one imagines as a fertility symbol, a healthy buxom figure like the Baubo. And yet the position of the hands directs attention to the organ of reproduction. It is like an invitation which is, at the same time, repellent. What could it possibly signify?

The name itself is not understood. If rendered in Gaelic it would be 'Sileadh na gCīoch', ie 'shedding (of liquid) from the breasts'. However in the absence of breasts from the figure, 'cīoch' might be taken as a misrepresentation of 'gīog', meaning hunkers; this might be more apposite, as it approximates to the squatting position of the figures: on their hunkers. A shedding of liquid from the hunkers? To take this as meaning urination is a little prosaic. Could it possibly refer to the activity of menstruation?

At this point in my musings, I came upon another reference to North Africa which was like a searchlight on the subject. This was the phenomenon of the Christian Gnostics. Gnosis means 'knowledge' or 'insight'. The word is applied to those Christians who relied on their own spiritual resources, their personal insights, to discover their relationship with God. This automatically placed them at loggerheads with the authority of the established Church which, naturally, wished to maintain a monopoly of the 'truth' and the graces by which people could achieve it. Gnostics were at the extreme end of a spectrum of belief which tended to disagree with the idea that the 'Church' was the sole mediator between God and Man. They further had a very jaundiced view of the world, considering it to be essentially evil and their aim was to separate the 'divine spark' from the material world. Among the Gnostic sects were my old friends the Manichaeans, the Cathars, the Mandeans and many others described as heretics. What intrigued me about some of these was a description of their rituals which suggested to me a direct connection with the Sheela na Gigs.

I first came across such a description of these in a book, *The Dead Sea Scrolls and the Christian Myth* by John Allegro who had been one of the first Western observers to be invited to study these scrolls when they were discovered. I spent many invigorating hours with him, listening as he described the 'cover-up' imposed by the Great Church on the early days of Christianity. He quoted Clement of Alexandria, speaking in the second century, as saying: 'not everything that is true need necessarily be divulged to all men'. He did not dismiss my speculation on the relationship between the Sheelas and the Gnostics, and brought to my attention a fourth-century bishop who had described the rituals of a Gnostic group called the Phibionites:

> The shameless ones have sexual intercourse and I am truly abashed to say what scandalous things they practise ... following coitus in uninhibited lust, they proceed to blaspheme Heaven itself. The man and woman take the ejaculated sperm in their hands, step forward, raise their eyes aloft and, with the defilement still on their hands, offer up prayers ... They then proceed to eat it in their infamous ritual, saying: This is the Body of Christ, and this is the Pascha (Passover Meal) through which our bodies suffer and are made to acknowledge

the passion of Christ. They behave similarly with a woman's menstrual blood: they collect from her the monthly blood of impurity, take it, eat it in a common meal and say: This is Christ's Blood.

Accounts like this were written by orthodox bishops who would naturally paint as lurid a description as possible of their opponents' activities. But there were many, equally disturbing accounts of 'agape' or love-feasts in which the male semen and the female blood would be mixed into a kind of cake and eaten. As John Allegro said: 'It must have been revolting,' but the aesthetic sense of true believers is not often finely developed.

I could easily imagine the male sexual function being included in religious ritual; phallic worship is one of the most ancient forms of religion. Was it possible that this function was what the Sheelas symbolized: the idea of the female producing her contribution to the sacred ritual? The principal import of John Allegro's argument was that sex and religion were intimately tied together. 'That is why,' he said, 'the Church is afraid of sex and has been for the past two thousand years.' He traced the rise of Gnostic belief through the Essenes – the authors of the Dead Sea Scrolls – right back to the Canaanites of Palestine. This was where, he said, the Phoenicians had come from, the same people who founded Carthage and had sailed north to the British Isles. He thought it not at all unlikely that they would have brought with them the secrets of their mystic cults. Carthage was much later a stronghold of Gnosticism.

North Africa was the centre of such cults right through the early Christian era. If my speculations were correct and these outlawed sects sought refuge along the Atlantic seaways, they would naturally have brought some of their more bizarre customs with them to Ireland. 'St Patrick' might have banished or converted Christians who subscribed to serpent worship but it would not be as easy to destroy the stone evidence of a cult which incorporated women into their rituals. Any successful Church has to take over a selection of the customs of the people it is evangelizing in order to get anywhere. Christianity has shown a genius for this process. The Sheela na Gigs must have represented a fairly deep-rooted belief for such a bizarre idea to be adopted and incorporated in the Orthodox Church's own buildings. I do not believe too much stress can be placed on the Sheela na Gigs. They are such an outrageously awkward phenomenon to fit into the standard interpretation of early Irish Christianity or any conventional account of the island that they are worth worrying at. Conventional accounts overlook the point that women were part and parcel of the monastic scene in Ireland; that even in saintly Clonmacnoise there is a carving of a Sheela na Gig; that the old Gaelic for a nun is 'cailleach' which can be translated as 'witch' or 'hag'; the original description in Gaelic of a 'nun's chapel' is 'temple of the hag'.

In these matters, Irish monasticism was clearly to be distinguished from the great monasteries of Europe where celibacy was introduced quite early. In the East, on the other hand, celibacy was not and is not mandatory for other than the very highest Church dignitaries. Once again, the island seemed to have more affinity with the East than the West. Even the objection that, apart from the Baubo, there are no examples of Sheelas apparent in North Africa did not discourage me from this idea. The Irish manuscript illuminations and stone crosses all incorporate Eastern ideas but emerge as something unique to the island; the islanders took these ideas and made of them their own. In their cultural as well as their economic structures of Christianity, they were much closer to the East than the West. It would not have been beyond the scope of craftsmen on the island to render as bizarre an idea as the Phibionite ritual into something as solid as a stone.

It is inevitable that if the Sheelas ever had a fundamental significance in the belief systems of this island – be they Gnostic, Orthodox, Christian, pagan or semi-pagan – the memory of such a device would gradually have been eroded by the ministrations of an officially celibate Western Church. What happens in a case like this is that the memory and meaning of such practices enter the people's folklore; this is then assumed to be of purely secular or pagan origin. But, as I have emphasized before, up to quite recent times everything in life, particularly peasant life, was articulated in a religious context. Every aspect of folk- lore has a religious origin, be it pagan or Christian.

There is an old belief that the way to stop a charging bull is for a woman to expose her buttocks to him. This is a polite form of an older belief that a woman could drive away the Devil by exposing her genitals. In Ireland, one of the 'pishrogues' attached to the Sheela was that it was a means of averting the evil eye. This was rooted in the idea that a man who had suffered the atten- tions of this evil eye could call on a woman to expose herself and thus cure his affliction. A belief in the curative properties of the Sheela is evi- denced by the custom of rubbing the limbs of carvings which are located at Holy Wells and scenes of 'Patterns'. Significantly, some of these 'Pattern' days fall on the feast of St Brigid. In some cases, the sign of the cross is made on the figure, a custom which is the exact counterpart of the early Christian custom of carving crosses on existing standing stones. The latter had clear phallic implications in pre-Christian Ireland.

In general, the attempts to locate the origin of the Sheelas in a continental European context are as unconvincing as the efforts to gloss over all the other awkward details in the personality of Ireland. Even the suggestion that Eastern influences were mediated through Southern Gaul has a relevance here. It was in this region of Southern France that the heresy of the Cathars flourished right up to the thirteenth century. That heresy was directly descended from the Manichaeans whom Augustine condemned in the fifth century for their profane rituals. Shortly before the crusading spirit brought the Anglo-Normans to Ireland, a major crusade was preached against these 'Albigensians' in the south of France.

Over the years that I was encountering all of these disparate aspects of Ireland, Europe, the Middle East and North Africa, the image that kept recurring to me was of a jigsaw puzzle. All of the pieces seemed to be present but the manner in which they were assembled, the accepted historical and geographical perspective, looked right only when viewed from one point of view: the central European perspective. From any other place, such as Conamara, on the edge of Europe, the pieces seemed to have been assembled by a child: some had the edges frayed awkwardly; there were, on closer examination, many pieces missing. Could the jigsaw be reassembled to make any more sense? Where, for example, would you place the centre: London, Paris, Madrid, Munich, Moscow? What did the world look like when Alexandria was its acknowledged centre? How did Europe appear to the Islamic or Chinese or Aztec Empires – if they ever thought about it. Fairly unimportant, I imagine.

The centre is obviously a shifting perspective, its movement directly related to power, or to the prejudice of whoever assembled the jigsaw. The achievement of power was, up to a few centuries ago, directly related to mobility by sea – the British Empire is a classic example. So why not look at the social and cultural characteristics of peoples from this perspective? The Spanish, French, Portuguese, Dutch, British all used the sea to acquire new territories and the new wealth with which to finance their squabbles in Europe. History has tended to concentrate on these local squabbles, so much so that Europeans have naturally assumed that these squabbles were what constituted the sum total of significant history.

It is, as you know by now, from a defiantly peripheral standpoint that I have chosen to return the compliment and view Europe, occasionally sourly, from 'the outside'. From this viewpoint, Europe itself rapidly retreats into a peripheral position.

What conception did, for instance, Hannibal have of Europe to see it as an easy target for an expedition in 218 BC? His exploits are still wondered at. He, a North African, could conceive of attacking Rome from the rear, from the north, the long way round via Spain, France and Switzerland. He could transport from Carthage an army 102,000 strong: 90,000 infantry, 12,000 of the famous Numidian cavalry, even thirty-seven elephants and bring them over the Pyrenees and the Alps and into the heart of the Roman Empire. He was so familiar with Europe that he could even recruit local European tribes on the way. Having arrived in Italy, and failed to take Rome, he could still spend the next twenty years dominating the countryside and harassing the towns – and this was after Rome had allegedly defeated the Carthaginians.

Where was the all-conquering Roman Empire if it could not evict such a nuisance as Hannibal from its own country? It suggests that this Empire was not as all-embracing, all-controlling as we have been led to believe. The latter impression is obviously based on the fact that the Romans left records, Hannibal did not.

When W.B. Yeats observed that 'things fall apart, the centre cannot hold', he predicted that the result would be a blood-red tide loosed upon the world. But he seemed to overlook that the 'centre' has usually been the cause of such blood-red tides. Nevertheless, one can sympathize with his dread of authority being dissipated to a situation of 'every man for himself and the devil take the hindmost'. On the other hand, just as aggressive central powers in their colonial mode invariably attribute the disorganization of a people to some fault inherent in the nature of that people, so the necessary dismantling of a centralized academic perspective may cause some heartburn but it is, in the end, worth it.

It is ironic that the worm's-eye view of history is beginning to emerge just as the world is once more being carved up into even larger blocs by Great Powers. Perhaps it is analogous to what G.B. Shaw, an Irishman, said about the nineteenth-century nature poets: that they only started to appreciate the beauty of the world when it was threatened by industrialization. As we find ourselves increasingly being fitted, modular-like, into a consumer world – be it as citizens of the US, the USSR, the EEC or any other conglomeration – we are forced to look desperately for evidence of our uniqueness as persons and peoples. But this should not prevent us – indeed, must encourage us – to admit at all times that every nation, big or small, is a concoction, an arbitrary mixture of cultures and races, each of whose constituent parts is indispensable to the overall flavour.

Bob Quinn
Carraroe, Conamara

# Sources of Reference

NB: Many of the following works were used throughout the research despite being mentioned only once below

## Chapter One

BRENNAN, MARTIN, *Boyne Valley Vision*, Dolmen Press, 1980.
BURTON, R.F., *Book of the Sword*, 1884.
GIRALDUS CAMBRENSIS, *The History and Topography of Ireland*, trans. J.J. O'Meara, Dolmen Press, 1982.
CARR, E.H., *What is History?*, Penguin, 1983.
COHANE, JOHN P., *The Key*, Turnstone Books, 1969.
*Collectanea de Rebus Hibirnicis 1786*, vol. 4, no. XIV.
DE COURCY IRELAND, JOHN, *Ireland and the Sea*, Cumann Merriman, 1983.
DELARGY, SEAMUS, *The Gaelic Story Teller*, quoted by T.K. Whitaker in an address to Antrim Historical Society.
EVANS, E.E. *Personality of Ireland*, Blackstaff, 1981.
GRAVES, ROBERT, *The White Goddess*, Faber and Faber, 1961.
KIEWE, H.E., *Civilization on Loan*, Alden and Mowbray, 1973.
LANE, WALTER D., studies, the Hibernian Antiquarian Society, autumn 1962.
MacNEILL, EOIN, *Phases of Irish History*, 1937.
RENFREW, COLIN, essay on 'Culture, Migration, Invasion Models in Prehistory', *Antiquity*, vol. XLII, no. 166, June 1986.
RYAN, MICHAEL, *Ireland's First Inhabitants*, Bull. Dept. of Foreign Affairs, no. 983, December 1981.
SCOTT, F.R., *Selected Poems*, Oxford University Press, 1966.
SPENSER, EDMUND, *View of the State of Ireland*, Ed. W.L. Renwick, Clarendon Press, 1970.
*Viking and Medieval Dublin*, National Museum Excavations, 1962–73.
WILSON, DAVID, *The New Archaeology*, New American Library, 1974.
WOODMAN, PETER, *The Mesolithic in Ireland*, British Archaeological Reports, 1978.

# Chapter Two

ACTON, CHARLES, 'Sean-nōs and the Arab Style', *Irish Times*, 4 November 1974.
BODLEY, SEOIRSE, *Technique and Structure in Sean-nōs Singing*, Ceol Tire, 1973.
CARPENTER, RHYS, *Beyond the Pillars of Hercules*, Tandem, 1973.
CORKERY, DANIEL, *The Hidden Ireland*, Gill and McMillan, 1970.
HAYES, JOHN R., *The Genius of Arabic Civilization*, MIT Press, 1978.
HIGGINS, MICHAEL D., 'Tyranny of Images', *The Crane Bag*, vol. 8, no. 2, 1984.
MILLMAN, LAWRENCE, *Our Like will not be Three Again*, Little Brown, 1977.
O'BAOILL, SEAN, *Traditional Singing in English*, Treoir, 1974.
O'BOYLE, SEAN, *Ogham: The Poet's Secret*, Dalton, 1980.
O'RIADA, SEAN, 'Our Musical Heritage', RTE, 1963.
O'ROURKE, BRIAN, *Blas Meala*, Irish Academic Press, 1985.
SCOTT, RICHARD J., *The Galway Hooker*, Ward River Press, 1983.

# Chapter Three

COSTELLO, CON, *Ireland and the Holy Land*, C. Goodliffe Neale, 1974.
EL-SAID and PARMAN, *Geometric Concepts in Islamic Art*, World of Islam Festival Publishing Co, 1976.
HENRY, FRANÇOISE, *Early Christian Irish Art*, Mercier Press, 1979.
JAMES, DAVID, *Celtic and Islamic Art*, Art About Ireland, 1979.
ROWAN, ERIC, Editor, *Art in Wales*, University of Wales Press, 1978.
RYAN, MICHAEL, Editor, *Treasures of Early Irish Art*, National Museum of Ireland, 1983.
SHEPPARD, PHILIP, *Byzantium*, Time-Life Institutions, 1978.
TALBOT RICE, DAVID, *Islamic Art*, Thames & Hudson, 1965.
YEATS, W.B., *Deirdre*, Collected Plays of W.B. Yeats, Macmillan, 1952.

# Chapter Four

BARNABY, HENRY, *The Sack of Baltimore*, Cork Historical and Archaeological Society, vol. LXXIV, no. 220.
BARNET, R.D., *Antiquity*, vol. XXXII, 1958.

CHAMBERS, ANNE, *Granuaile*, Wolfhound Press, 1979.
DE COURCY IRELAND, JOHN, *The Corsairs of North Africa*, Mariners Mirror.
HARDEN, DONALD, *The Phoenicians*, Thames and Hudson, 1962.
INGLIS, H.D., *Ireland in 1834*, Whittaker & Co, 1835.
JOYCE, P.W., *A Social History of Ancient Ireland*, Gresham, 1913.
KENNEY, JAMES, *Sources for the Early History of Ireland*, Columbia University Press, 1929.
MITCHELL, DAVID, *Pirates*, Dial Press, New York, 1976.
*Navigatio Sancti Brendani*, trans. J.J. O'Meara, Mercier, 1971.
RAMIN, JACQUES, *The Periplus of Hanno*, British Archaeological Reports, 1976.
SEVERIN, TIM, *The Brendan Voyage*, Arrow Books, 1979.

# Chapter Five

BOWEN, E.G., *Saints, Seaways and Settlements*, University of Wales Press, 1969.
DANIEL, GLYN, *Megalith Builders of Western Europe*, Hutchinson, 1958.
*Folk Life*, vol. 1, no. 63, Folk Life Society, Cardiff.
HARDING, D.W., *Prehistoric Europe*, Phaidon Press, 1978.
*The Iron Age in the Irish Sea Province*, CBA Research Report 9, 1978.
MOURANT and WATKINS, 'Blood Groups in Wales', *Heredity*, vol. 6, 1952.
OWEN, TREFOR M., *Welsh Folk Customs*, Welsh National Museum, 1959.

# Chapter Six

BENOIT, F., 'La Stele de Maaziz', Bulletin de la Société de Préhistorique du Maroc, 1932.
BERTRAND, ANDRE, *Tribus Berberus de Haut Atlas*, Edita. Vilo. 1977.
COFFEY, GEORGE, *Newgrange*, Dolphin Press, 1977.
GAILEY, ALAN, *Irish Folk Drama*, Mercier, 1969.
GALWASH, AHMED A., *The Religion of Islam*, Cairo, 1956.
KHALDOUN, IBN, *The Muqaddimah*, trans. Franz Rosenthal, Routledge & Kegan Paul, 1967.
MaCADAM, ROBERT, 'Is the Irish Language Spoken in Africa?' *JRSAI* vol VII.

MACKEY, GEORGE, 'Celtic Tribes in Morocco' *Caledonian Medical Journal*, vol. VII, no. 5, January 1908.

MAVOR, JAMES W., 'The Riddle of Mxorah' *Almogaren* VII, 1976.

NORRIS, H.T. *The Berbers in Arabic Literature*, Longman, 1982.

SHEEHY, JEANNE, *Rediscovery of Ireland's Past*, Thames and Hudson, 1980.

SOUVILLE, GEORGE, 'Engraved Steles from Western Morocco', *Atlas Préhistorique du Maroc Atlantique*.

## Chapter Seven

ARDEN, JOHN, *Silence Among the Weapons*, Methuen, 1982.

*The Celts*, ed. Joseph Raftery, Mercier Press, 1978.

DANAHER, KEVIN, 'Irish Folk Tradition and the Celtic Calendar', *The Celtic Consciousness*, Dolmen Press, 1982.

DE PAOR, LIAM, 'The Art of the Celtic Peoples', *The Celtic Consciousness*, Dolmen Press, 1982.

DILLON, MYLES, *The Irish Language*, Early Irish Society, 1954.

FLOWER, ROBIN, *The Irish Tradition*, Clarendon Press, 1978.

GREENE, DAVID, *Early Irish Society*, Sign of the Three Candles, 1954.

HENRY, P.L., *Anglo-Irish Word Chants in Ulster Dialects*, Ulster Folk Museum, 1964.

JACKSON, K.H., *A Celtic Miscellany*, Penguin, 1971.

JONES, MORRIS, 'Pre-Aryan Syntax in Insular Celtic', *The Welsh People*, London, 1900.

MURPHY, GERARD, *Saga and Myth in Ancient Ireland*, Three Candles Press, 1961.

O'DANACHAIR, CAOMHIN, 'A Celtic Origin of the Irish Folk Tradition?' *Arizona State University Anthropological Research Papers No. 27*, 1982.

PIGGOTT, STUART, *The Druids*, Penguin, 1975.

POWELL, T.G.E., *The Celts*, Thames and Hudson, 1980.

RAFTERY, JOSEPH, Editor, *The Celts*, Mercier, 1978.

SHARKEY, JOHN, *Celtic Mysteries*, Avon, 1975.

SITWELL, N.H.S., *The World the Romans Knew*, Hamish Hamilton, 1984.

WAGNER, HEINRICH, *Common Problems Concerning the Early Languages of the British Isles and the Iberian Peninsula*, Universidad de Salamanca, 1976; 'Near Eastern and African Connections with the Celtic World', *The Celtic Consciousness*, Dolmen Press, 1982.

# Chapter Eight

CAESAR, JULIUS, *The Conquest of Gaul,* trans. S.A. Handford, Penguin, 1951.

*Course of Irish History,* eds. Moody and Martin, Mercier Press, 1967.

DANIEL, NORMAN, *The Arabs and Medieval Europe,* Longman, 1979.

'Ireland and the Sea', papers presented at the Merriman Summer School, Lahinch, 1982.

LEWIS, ARCHIBALD, R., *The Northern Seas,* Princeton, 1958.

MANSOOR, M., *The Story of Irish Orientalism,* 1944.

# Chapter Nine

BURCKHARDT, TITUS, *Moorish Culture in Spain,* Allen & Unwin, 1972.

FOSS, MICHAEL, *Chivalry,* Joseph, 1975.

LANE POOLE, STANLEY, 'The Moors in Spain', Khoyats Oriental Reprint, no. 23, Beirut, 1962.

MORAN, DERMOT, *Johannes Scottus Eriugena,* Art About Ireland, 1979.

NORDENFALK, CARL, *Celtic and Anglo-Saxon Painting,* Chatto & Windus, 1977.

O'MEARA, JOHN J., *Eriugena,* Mercier Press, 1969.

RYAN, MICHAEL, *The Derrynaflan Chalice and Other Early Irish Chalices,* National Museum of Ireland, 1983.

STANFORD, W.B., 'Towards a History of Classical Influences in Ireland', *PRIA,* vol. 70, sec. C, no. 3, 1970.

TRILLING, JAMES, *The Roman Heritage,* Textile Museum, Washington, 1982.

YONGE, CHARLOTTE, M., *Christians and Moors of Spain,* Macmillan, 1903.

# Chapter Ten

*Amazigh,* Quarterly Review, Rabat, 1982.

BARING-GOULD, S., *Curious Myths of the Middle Ages,* Jupiter Books, 1975.

BAYLEY, HAROLD, *Lost Language of Symbolism*, Williams and Northgate, 1951.

BOSWELL, W.P., 'Irish Wizards in the Woods of Ethiopia', unpublished thesis.

CARNEY, JAMES, *The Impact of Christianity*, Early Irish Society, Mercier Press, 1954.

DANAHER, KEVIN, *In Ireland Long Ago*, Mercier, 1962.

FALLON, NIALL, *The Armada in Ireland*, Stamford Maritime, 1978.

FELL, BARRY, *America B.C.*, Wallaby, 1978.

O'FARRELL, PADRAIC, *Folk Tales of the Irish Coast*, Mercier, 1978.

O'SIOCHAIN, P.A., *A Journey into Lost Time*, Foillsiuchan Eireann Teo, 1984.

PURCE, JILL, *The Mystic Spiral*, Thames & Hudson, 1974.

RANELAGH, E.L., *The Past We Share*, Quartet Books, 1979.

SPANUTH, JURGEN, *Atlantis of the North*, Grabert Verlag, 1976.

WALSH, R.A., *A Residence at Constantinople*, 1838.

# Chapter Eleven

ATIYA, AZIZ S., *The Copts and Christian Civilization*, University of Utah, 1979.

BEDE, *A History of the English Church and People*, Penguin, 1983.

BURY, J.B., *Life of St Patrick*, Macmillan, 1905.

CAMPBELL, JOSEPH, 'Peripheries of the Indo-European World', *The Celtic Consciousness*, Dolmen Press, 1982.

DE PAOR, MAIRE and LIAM, *Early Christian Ireland*, Thames & Hudson, 1971.

EMMERY, W.B., *Archaic Egypt*, Penguin, 1961.

HAMELL, P.J., *Patrology*, Maynooth, 1963.

INGE, W.R., *The Church in the World*, Longman Green, 1927.

JOHNSON, PAUL, *A History of Christianity*, Penguin, 1980.

PAGEL, ELAINE, *The Gnostic Gospels*, Pelican, 1982.

RICHARDSON, HILARY, 'Art in Ireland in the Eighth Century', paper delivered at Salzburg, September 1984.

STOKES, G.T., *Ireland and the Celtic Church*, Hodder & Stoughton, 1886.

THOMAS, CHARLES, *Britain and Ireland in Early Christian Times*, Thames & Hudson, 1971.

VIAUD, GERARD, *Pratique Populaires Communes aux Coptes et aux Celtes*, Sociétié d'Archaeologie, Copte T XXIII, Cairo, 1981.

WAND, J.W.C., *A History of the Early Church*, Methuen, 1977.

WHITE, N.J.D., *Latin Writings of St Patrick*, SPCK, 1918.

# Chapter Twelve

BIELER, L., *Ireland, Harbinger of the Middle Ages,* Oxford University Press, 1963.
GUITTON, JEAN, *Great Heresies and Church Councils,* Harvill, 1963.
KIEWE, H.E., *The Sacred History of Knitting,* ANI, Oxford, 1967.
LACARRIERE, JACQUES, *The God Possessed,* Allen & Unwin, 1963.
LANE POOLE, STANLEY, *A History of Egypt,* Methuen, 1925.

# Chapter Thirteen

ALLEGRO, JOHN M., *The Dead Sea Scrolls and the Christian Myth,* Abacus, 1981.
ANDERSEN, JORGEN, *The Witch on the Wall,* Allen & Unwin, 1977.
JERMAN, JAMES A., 'Sheela na Gigs of the British Isles', Journal of Co Louth Archaeological and Historical Society, vol. XX, no. 1, 1981.
MERRIMAN, BRIAN, *The Midnight Court,* Mercier, 1982.
O'CONNOR, MORRIS, W., *Hannibal,* Putnams, 1897.
RUDOLPH, KURT, *Gnosis,* T & T Clark, Edinburgh, 1983.
RYLEY SCOTT, G., *Phallic Worship,* Panther, 1970.
WIER, ANTHONY, *Exhibitionists and Related Carvings in the Irish Midlands,* Irish Midland Studies, Old Athlone Society, 1980.